"That Kind Can Never Change!" ...Can They... ?

One man's struggle with his homosexuality.

by
Victor J. Adamson

Huntington House Publishers

Huntington House Publishers
P.O. Box 53788
Lafayette, Louisiana 70505

PRINTED IN THE UNITED STATES OF AMERICA.

Library of Congress Card Catalog Number 00-102924
ISBN 1-56384-175-4

The attitude expressed in the title is held by many Christians today in regard to the homosexual in particular but could also extend to those of any "socially unacceptable" besetting sin or lifestyle. This title is based upon an unfortunate direct *pro*nouncement *against* and *de*nouncement of the author by a local pastor one year after the author's conversion; a pastor who just could not believe that even God could change someone like the homosexual. The same point was made repeatedly by a local elder of the author's own church two years after his conversion.

Such Christians need to understand that their faith may be no more than a mere "*form* of godliness, denying the *power* thereof."

May these people come to know and understand our God as mighty to save; even "to the uttermost." "Whosoever" includes the homosexual.

(King James English from Hebrews 7:25)

Contents

SECTION ONE
The "Gay" Life/A Misnomer

SECTION TWO
Looking Back at Childhood

SECTION THREE
Those Troubled Teen Years

SECTION FOUR
Having It All; and Then the Fall

SECTION FIVE
The Long Journey Home

SECTION SIX
Home at Last

Preface

This book is written primarily for the homosexual, sin sick and desperate for deliverance. Throughout the book, in dealing with the issue of sinners in general and the homosexual in particular, the words "he," "him," and "his" are used in the generic sense, as in the Bible: "So God created man in His own image, in the image of God created he him; male and female created he them" (Gen. 1:27). In this book, these usually masculine pronouns are frequently used in the generic and inclusive sense, representing male and female as in "mankind," the species; not for the purpose of excluding the female gender of sinners in general and homosexual's in particular, but to allow for the ease of writing and the ease of reading.

Whether the homosexual is in denial, latent, "in the closet," openly gay, "married," militant, or even a "flaming queen"; whether he believes to have been born "gay" or conditioned to be gay, my testimony is to show that it does not really matter. If someone is drowning, it matters not whether he *fell* into the water, *fell asleep* in the water, *jumped* into the water, or was *thrown* into the water. The bottom line is that he needs a life guard, a savior. This manuscript is meant to arouse the victim to awareness of his need and then point him to the Lifeguard, his Savior Jesus Christ.

Secondly, this book is for the family and friends of homosexuals who just cannot understand what went wrong; who grieve over the lost condition of those whom they love; who feel helpless, not knowing how to show them the way out. A proper understanding of the power of Jesus to save His people from their sins should be a real comfort and a weapon against the enemy.

Thirdly, this book is for pastors and counselors, to assist them in their work of seeking to save the lost.

This book is for *any* sin sick soul who may not yet have discovered that our Jesus is mighty to save. "In all ages, and in every nation, those who believe that Jesus can and will save them personally from sin [their own besetting sin of whatever nature] are the elect and chosen of God, His peculiar treasure" (*Review and Herald,* 1 August 1893). This book is for the "whosoevers." For "*Whosoever* believeth in Him, should not perish" (John 3:16).

Revelation 12:11 tells us that we overcome the accuser of the brethren by the blood of the Lamb, and by the word of our testimony. The goal of this book is to expose the lie of Satan who charges that it is impossible to overcome the sin of homosexuality or any other besetting sin. He has foisted upon Christianity a form of godliness, denying the power thereof. To believe "that kind (any kind) of sinner can never change," or be changed, is to deny the power of God Himself. "For it is God which worketh in you both to will and to do of his good pleasure" (Phil. 2:13). And we can be "confident of this very thing, that he which hath begun a good work in you will perform it until the day of Jesus Christ" (Phil. 1:6). May the accuser of the brethren be overcome, and may the love and power of God be vindicated, at least to some degree through the word of my testimony.

Victor J. Adamson

Acknowledgments

Special thanks go to my parents who are aware of the writing of this book and give their full approval. Knowing that my testimony, painful at times, involves many of their own mistakes and failings as parents, of which they, too, are painfully aware; this book in a sense becomes their testimony as well.

Their statement: "Let the chips fall where they may. If this book can help even one soul better understand himself and find his way to Christ, that is really all that matters."

The same heavenly Father who came looking for me, His lost sheep, has also worked mightily in the hearts and lives of my parents and family who are willing now to bear the public scrutiny that such a book as this might incite.

However, in an attempt to spare them and others any undue pain and embarrassment, I have chosen to alter the names of the innocent, the guilty, and the repentant, and some of the identifying details.

Special appreciation also must be expressed to others of my family and church family who have been so supportive of me in my new life in Christ.

Special gratitude goes also to my dear wife, the love of my life, who has followed the ups and downs of my life since childhood, and yet, trusting in the power of the Re-Creator God to save this sinner from his lifestyle of sin, was willing to become one with me in love, in life, and in ministry. Through the proofreading of the original manuscript, she has learned more about me than I ever wished anyone to know, yet she loves me still and remains by my side to uplift and uphold.

May God and God alone be glorified!

Introduction

Do you have a son or daughter, a brother or sister, or a special loved one of any relation or of no relation who is wandering in the Valley of the Lost Sheep? Are you yourself, perhaps, wavering in your own personal relationship with Christ, your Creator and Savior?

The purpose of this book is to share with you what Christ has done in my life to save me from a downward spiral that was leading me in *this* life to ultimate destruction, and even worse, to eternal destruction. It is my prayer that at least some portion of this personal testimony may help you, or someone you know, avoid some of the pitfalls that I have experienced. If my testimony is able to help even one person come to know Christ more fully and to accept Him without reservation, then the mission of this book has been accomplished.

Though expressed to some degree, it is not the object of this book to detail the feelings, emotions, romantic fantasies, and sexual behavior of a homosexual, which might only serve to glorify the work of Satan and his counterfeit for happiness, and to feed the appetite of the unconverted. I wish not to in any way encourage the tendencies toward homosexual behavior in one who may be either in denial, latent, "in the closet," or openly gay. Neither do I wish to offend or repulse the reader who may *not* have any bent toward homosexuality within himself, but who might be reading to be informed, and/or for the benefit of someone else in need.

Therefore, the details of my life of sin are not the subject of this book. Rather, my endeavor is to help others through my own autobiography, to understand the homosexual, to have

13

love and compassion for him, and, most of all, to show that through the grace of God there is hope, blessed hope, for his redemption *from* the lifestyle which I now believe to be so out of harmony with God's purpose for the creation of man and woman in the very beginning. In facing eternal realities, I have come to realize that though the "gay" life may be gay at times, it promises no lasting, genuine love, joy, or peace. On the contrary, it is fraught with much anxiety, fear, frustration, suspicion, depression, and despair. Neither does it offer one the assurance of being able to face an all-loving, merciful, yet perfectly just God in the judgment. The writing of this book has been a roller coaster ride of emotion for me. As memories have been resurrected from the dead, this work has evoked both joy and laughter, but also shame and remorse, much pain, and frequent tears. The process of writing out this testimony has been a very difficult one, for what God has promised to bury in the depths of the sea, I have had to go after as a deep sea diver would go after the sunken wreckage of the Titanic.

    May sin someday soon forever rest in peace.

                                                    Victor J. Adamson

SECTION ONE

The "Gay" Life/
A Misnomer

One

A Rude Awakening

"Where am I?" I wondered. "What's happening? What am I doing here?"

I seemed to be hallucinating or something. Everything seemed to be out of focus. The people around me seemed somewhat familiar. Wait! I know who they are. No, I don't.

"What is going on here?" I asked myself. "Am I drugged? Have I had too much to drink again? I can't remember. Maybe I've been smoking pot."

The world seemed to whirl around me in darkness, coming into focus, then, just as quickly blurring into some strange collage of familiar and unfamiliar people, surroundings, and events.

"And why is it so dark, so gloomy?"

While trying to make sense out of what was going on around me, I did not at first notice what was going on above me. I was too distracted by all the clamor and confusion that seemed to be going on in every direction I looked.

Suddenly, the darkness was pierced by a great light coming from above. All eyes looked toward the source of the light, directing my gaze to follow. In horror I realized that time had come to an end as I gazed into the heavens and saw coming in clouds of glory Jesus, surrounded by all the heavenly host. I could not look into His eyes, for I was overwhelmed with the awareness of my life of shame and degradation.

"I'm lost!" I cried out. "Lost! Forever lost!"

The reality of my eternal destiny filled me with a horror that words, at least my words, can never adequately express.

In abject terror, I sat bolt upright in bed. The terrible scene of glory was gone. I was once again in wonderful darkness, safe from that penetrating gaze of Jesus as He came to claim His own.

In a cold sweat, I muttered, "Thank God, it was only a dream! I still have time . . . ."

Eventually, I settled back down into bed. Freckles, my twenty-five pound cat, mustered up enough courage to jump back upon the bed from which he had no doubt been catapulted by my sudden rude awakening. As was his habit, he climbed onto my legs, walked cautiously up my body and onto my chest, purring loudly as if to warm me up so that I would let him sleep with me. Sticking his cold little nose up to mine in his funny little greeting, he collapsed onto my chest, all twenty-five pounds, making it difficult for me to breathe. His back end slowly slid off to the left, then the rest of him followed, and he was soon sound asleep next to me with his head on my shoulder, purring peacefully in his slumber.

"Oh, for the peace and security of that cat!" I thought as I tried to relax and go back to sleep, haunted by "the dream." This was not the first time I had had such a rude awakening, for "the dream" was a recurring one, although not every night, not every week, not even every month. But for several years, when least expecting it, the dream would recur. The setting was usually different each time, but always the climax was the same—Jesus coming in the clouds of glory and my terror as I experienced the horror of being lost. Awakened each time with a jolt, I tried to shrug it all off as just another dream—a nightmare. Though sleep would finally return, I was without the peace and security that I longed to have.

"But why couldn't I have peace?" I wondered. I had not chosen to be gay, as so many Christians had suggested to me. "I was born this way," I reasoned. Therefore, I was not responsible for who and what I was. I was God's creation, and if He had not wanted me to be gay (homosexual), then He wouldn't have made me this way. If being gay was a choice, I would never have made that choice, for with it came the consequences of hurting those I loved, the break up of my home, the loss of my children, alienation from my family and friends and church, the scorn and ridicule of the general public. It was all God's fault," I consoled myself.

As far as choices were concerned, I had made all the right choices. I had chosen a Christian education for myself. I had chosen to be a student missionary for two years in the Far East. I had chosen to study theology and pre-med preparatory to become a medical missionary some day. I had chosen to marry a Christian girl, and to have little Christian children. But eventually, no longer able to deny to myself who and what I really was inside, I had "accepted" being homosexual, and, in extreme frustration, turned my back on family, friends, God, and everything I had worked for, and entered into the gay life "rightfully" giving God all the credit (or blame).

So there! Now I should feel good about myself. But why did I keep having this dream? And why did I always wake up terrified with the feeling of being eternally lost? Was I deceiving myself? How did I really turn out to be this way?

With all these thoughts running through my mind, I finally drifted off into a fitful sleep.

Two

Is That All There Is . . . ?

Morning always seemed to come too soon. And the next morning after "the dream" was no exception. Very carefully I slipped out of bed so as not to disturb Freckles the cat. I had developed the skill of sleeping in such a way that my bed looked almost undisturbed in the morning, thus making it very quick and easy to put it in order in the morning. However, this morning it was a mess!

I dismissed the dream of the previous night and quickly went about my business of readying myself for the day. Being in marketing, I was on call for appointments, which usually came no earlier than late morning. So I had time to go through my daily morning workout routine. It is very important to most gays to remain as young and attractive as humanly possible for as long as possible. And I adhered to this principle religiously. Body building for bulk was of no real interest to me, but body shaping was of utmost importance. To look lean and athletic was to look good on the beach, in the work place, on the streets, and especially on the dance floors in the gay bars and nightclubs.

"Hello, Baby!" came the morning greeting from the living room.

"Hello, Baby yourself!" I chuckled as I paraded into the living room to then be greeted by a shrill wolf whistle that would flatter the ego of any self-respecting, self-loving, self-centered human being.

However, as it was coming from my little buddy, a Mexican parrot, I could only laugh with amusement. He certainly made it easy, though, to forget my troubles at times. At other times, he was pretty good at getting me into trouble. Like the time I was out on the patio bending over and watering my plants with Baby on my shoulder. I disinterestedly noticed the form of a young lady walking by, and so did Baby, but not with disinterest.

"Hello, Baby!" he called out loudly. Then he let out his best shrill wolf whistle. I jumped up in embarrassment. She jerked around in surprised amusement, only to see me sheepishly pointing to the parrot on my shoulder. With a knowing laugh she proceeded on her way, and Baby got a little scolding.

Whenever I would sit down to play my grand piano, Baby's behavior became very strange. He had come to live with me as an adult parrot already trained. It was a mystery to me why he would always start weeping and wailing whenever I played the piano. Everyone else praised my talent, but not Baby. He kept me humble. Why, he'd even cover his head with his wings and cry as though his heart was breaking. Perhaps my beautiful music brought back some heartbreak experience in his own life. I would never know.

I would get so tickled at this odd behavior that I couldn't help but laugh. That would start Baby laughing. The more he laughed, the more I laughed, resulting in a real laugh-in session. Obviously, Baby was the life of every party at my house.

I really enjoyed my pets. Ricky and Lucy were my lop-eared rabbits. I had to rename them, though, because one day Ricky had babies! So, she became "Ricki," and "Lucy" was modified to the masculine, Italian "Luci" (pronounced Lu-chee).

Fred and Ethel were my big white ducks. I had them from three days after hatching. So to them I was "Big Daddy Duck." They loved to swim in a little kiddie pool I bought for them. And they would follow behind me on my walks around the little private community. To the entertainment of the neighbors, if I managed to get too far ahead of them on the way home, they would put their little "waddles" in high gear, flap their wings to help accelerate, and quack out to me as loudly as they could while catching up with me.

At Thanksgiving, Fred and Ethel disappeared out of my fenced in backyard. I later discovered that a trespasser had captured them and taken them home for Thanksgiving dinner. He might as well have kidnaped my children! That's how incensed and violated I felt.

My, the world could be so cruel! Where was God on days like that? Where was justice? Where was mercy? My blame always tended to focus on God. I never thought to give Him credit for the good things in my life. And I never seemed to blame Satan for the bad. Everything was God's fault!

Tiffany Rose was my Schnauzer and very loyal friend and companion. Even in her old age she was a show stopper with her tricolor perfect markings of charcoal, silver, and cream. I kept her perfectly groomed for her own comfort, and, of course, for my own vanity. Never had anyone shown me more unconditional love than that little pooch. Her loving, doting brown eyes were almost human and so trusting, usually following my every move, unless, of course, she happened to be sleeping, which she seemed to do a lot these days. Surrounded by all this love and devotion, why did I still feel so lonely, and incomplete?

Oh, well, no time to think about that now. I needed to make sure I had breakfast down before the phone rang with a sales lead to follow up. Being a top salesman was a challenge I thoroughly enjoyed. I took my work seriously, for sales is a very competitive occupation. With my success came respect and acceptance, something that I seemed to really crave. I was not effeminate, or, in gay lingo, what one would call a "flaming queen." On the contrary, I consciously prided myself on being a man. Though I never flaunted my homosexuality, a few people who I worked with, and for, had me figured out for other reasons. But they were not fazed by it, at least they never seemed to be. I had sharpened my skills of being diplomatic, cheerful, industrious, and positive in outlook. It seemed that in the work place I was always appreciated and very well liked.

Scarfing down a couple of boiled eggs and some fruit, I grabbed my cup of coffee and went off to get dressed for business. No sooner had I gotten dressed than the phone rang, and I was off to an appointment some thirty miles away.

*   *   *   *   *

My sales job was very well suited to my lifestyle, for it allowed me to sleep in mornings after late nights of partying. Quite often my final appointment would be near some popular gay hang out. My sales experience had afforded me the opportunity to become well acquainted with these hangouts in five adjacent southern California counties. I would attempt to wrap up my appointments by 9:30 P.M. at the latest. That gave me time to grab a bite to eat and then arrive at a gay bar at just the right time.

It was important to not arrive too early at these places, because you might appear to be too anxious to meet someone new, in other words, "desperate." If you arrived real late, chances are you would have missed the best opportunities. So, 10:30 or 11:00 was just about the perfect time to make an appearance.

To be honest, bar hopping really became quite a bore and even down right depressing at times. No matter where I went, it was really the same old thing: drinking, smoking, and dancing to the beat; inhaling "poppers" on the dance floor to really get a rush, diminish inhibitions, and enhance the mood for sensual dancing; a little marijuana sometimes; and occasionally a little snorting of cocaine; getting hit upon by all the wrong types; and going home frustrated because "Mr. Right" ended up leaving with someone else!

What I really wanted in the gay life was a long-term relationship; a "marriage," so to speak. I wanted a "normal" life in which I could pursue a career, spend more time with my music, and just relax at home with a companion in a secure lifetime relationship. I participated in various sporting interests that I wanted to keep up with: hang gliding, ice skating, roller skating, biking, running, snow skiing. All of these interests, though pursued, took a back seat to finding fulfillment in the gay social life when not in a monogamous relationship.

I had been "married," so to speak, twice by now in my gay life. In fact, I had just terminated my second long-term gay relationship. Angelo was much younger than I and beautiful to behold; with his black curly hair, olive "Italian" complexion, vivid green eyes, and quick winning smile. We had been virtually married for five years, had a joint checking account, and even purchased a home together. Very outgoing, he was always the life of the party and usually managed to be the center of attention, deliberately.

But there was another side to Angelo that was not easily seen outside a relationship. The longer we were together, the more difficult it became to co-exist. I was very particular about the appearance of our home. But he was eccentric! If I got up from the sofa during a TV commercial break, I would come back to find him fluffing the pillows as if I was not to sit back down and muss the furniture! Upon my returning the TV Guide to the coffee table after using it, he would reach over and adjust its position so that it was exactly the way he had placed it. This type of compulsive behavior worked to undermine our comfort with one another. Actually, it downright got on my nerves. I got to where I would intentionally frustrate his efforts at keeping our house looking like his idea of a showcase. You might say that I became an instigator of some of his frustrations, because I had no sympathy for that kind of senseless behavior. I could be an ornery cuss if pushed far enough.

Angelo also became extremely possessive and jealous to the point that every time I wanted to pursue one of my own interests that he did not share, especially my hang gliding, he made life very difficult. Just being myself became a challenge to our relationship. He was a restless soul, and his idea of a good time was usually partying, bar hopping together, actually anything where he could be the focus of attention. Of course, we both liked taking in movies and rock concerts, and eating out at gay restaurants.

Angelo had a violent temper, and on numerous occasions had physically assaulted me, which eventually killed my love for him. I was not one to react with physical violence myself. It was against my nature. However, on one incident in Palm Springs his behavior was so bad in the middle of the night in a trailer park that I balled up my fist and planted one on his jaw and sent him reeling. He didn't know I was capable, (well, neither did I), and it sobered him up to the point that we could at least make it through the night.

I remember having a conversation with God about this time; one of the very few in many years. Usually I was blaming Him. But this time I prayed, "God, if you will get me out of this relationship, out of this mess, I *promise* I will go straight and never have another homosexual experience for the rest of my life."

My prayer was very much like the "old covenant" at Sinai. The stiff-necked, hard-hearted, fickle children of Israel had done the exact same thing when they *promised,* "All that the Lord hath spoken we will do" (Exodus 19:8). Before God could even get the written word back to them from the mount, they were partying down around an idol of gold right before His very eyes!

By apparent mutual agreement, eventually, Angelo and I sold our home and went our separate ways. Contrary to the popular song, breaking up was *not* so very hard to do after all. Later I learned that I had broken his heart, but he was too proud to reveal his true feelings, wanting me to believe our breakup was really his idea.

Now, totally oblivious to the promise I had made to the Lord, here I was, "free at last," and actively looking for some-one else to fill the void left in my life. Of course, that meant for me many one night stands, or "tricks" as we called them, before finding "Mr. Right." And how long would that search have to go on?

Is this what the rest of my life would be like? Being in and out of relationships? One night stands? "Tricking" for instant gratification? Surely life is meant to be more than this.

The words of that old Peggy Lee song so adequately ex-pressed my sentiments and frustrations: "Is that all there is? Is that all there is? If it is, my friend, then let's keep dancing. Let's bring out the booze and have a ball."

And so it was with my life, at least at that time.

Looking back on my young life which had seemed so full of promise, I queried, "How in the world did I ever end up in this lifestyle? What went wrong?"

— SECTION TWO —

Looking Back at Childhood

Three

Loss of Innocence and Childhood Antics

I was born into a Christian home to Christian parents, the fourth of six children, including my older half brother and sister who did not usually live with us. My brother Jake was one year older than I, and we had two younger sisters, Katie Rose and Carol Lynn within the next three years.

My father had been raised on the farm by well meaning, but harshly strict parents. Their home was full of love, but not without serious flaws. He was the youngest of five children. His mother showed open favoritism and partiality to one of his older brothers who died in a plane crash in early manhood. Until the day of her own death, she grieved at the mention of his name as if the tragedy had only just occurred.

His father was a small man who walked tall and carried a big stick, figuratively speaking. He would tolerate no monkey business in his children, and was physically abusive in his discipline of them, using as his primary instrument of punishment his big, black razor strap. In later years, though, as the Grandpa I knew, he was the ultimate tease and prankster himself. Although greatly feared by his children in childhood, he was dearly beloved and respected by all in his old age.

My mother was the oldest of three children, raised near the city by a father who loved them but who had no skills in child rearing. An intolerant, strong disciplinarian, he physically and emotionally abused his children into their late teens. My mother's mother so highly respected her husband that she was blind to his faults, to the detriment of her own children at times.

My father had first married at the age of seventeen, fathered two children, and, while in the military during World War II, was divorced by his wife who had fallen for another man. He suffered a nervous breakdown over the trauma and received a medical discharge from the Navy.

Several years later, he met my mother while in a Christian college in the south where he was studying to become a pastor. After one semester, they were engaged, and were then married the following summer. He was unable to further his education, especially when four children came along within the short period of five years. So he worked as a dairyman and farmer.

We moved frequently in those early years. By the time I was 4-years-old, we were living on a farm in the south. My parents wanted to keep their children protected from the corruptions of the world, and farm life in the country seemed to be the best way. But even in this environment, dangers were lurking.

While Daddy worked out in the fields, we boys enjoyed being with him on occasion. Watching the big farm equipment plowing, cultivating, harvesting, bailing hay, and so forth, was really great fun and quite an adventure for us at the ages of four and five.

One day while Daddy was harvesting with a combine, we were out in the fields with him. When the grain bin filled up on the combine, he emptied it into a truck driven by one of the young farm hands. While my brother rode on the combine with Daddy, I rode along in the truck with this teenager. Between dumps, he parked in the shade of a tree waiting for Daddy to signal when the combine bin was full.

An idle mind is the devil's workshop, and during one of those long waits, this teenage driver decided to take advantage of my young innocence and naivete. At the tender young age of four I was introduced to perverted sexual behavior. Embarrassed, traumatized, and in a state of shock, I tried to pretend that nothing had happened.

One might think that any "normal" 4-year-old would have

gone straight to Mommy or Daddy and tattled. Not this child. Feeling dirty and guilty, I suppressed the incident in my mind and determined to never tell. Though I was the victim of this perverted sexual behavior, I, a child of four, believed myself to somehow be the responsible culprit. I determined that Mommy and Daddy were to never find out what I had done.

*   *   *   *   *

In the years that followed, my childhood on the surface seemed normal enough. I was basically a good child, but participated in the typical sibling rivalry. With my brother being only one year older than I was, I found myself constantly measuring myself against him and competing with him where I thought I had a chance to come out ahead.

We had recently moved from the farm to a home in the suburbs of a southern city. I was almost five and my brother had just turned six. One evening just as it was getting dark, we sat out in front of our house on a hill overlooking the road below and decided to throw rocks over the oncoming vehicles. That soon got to be boring, so we decided to see who could be the first to score a *hit!*

Lucky me!

But as we heard the crack of the windshield followed by the screech of the braking tires, we suddenly realized the seriousness of the situation we had just created.

Jake and I ran to the house as fast as our little legs would take us, flew through the front door, tore through the little house, and disappeared under the bed in our bedroom. With bated breath we waited and hoped our sin would not find us out. But in just a moment or so, we heard a knocking at the door, then Mamma answering the door (bless her heart), not having a clue as to what was in store.

It must be understood that Mamma was so timid and shy that when Daddy asked her to marry him, all she could do was giggle. Poor Mamma! With little Katie and Carol hanging onto and hiding behind her skirt, she opened the door to find herself facing—*a police officer!* He informed her that he had been driving home with his son sitting in the front seat beside him when, suddenly, this big rock just fell from the sky right in front of her house and shattered the windshield of his car right in front of his little boy's face. Fortunately, no one was injured! He knew there had been witnesses who could help solve this mystery, for he had seen two little boys, apparently frightened by the freak accident themselves, running into her house. Perhaps they could be of some assistance in sorting out the details of what had happened . . . ?

Mamma was mortified! Suddenly the behavior of her two little cherubs just moments before began to make sense. Her face turned every shade of beet red in the heat of the moment. She had no explanation to give the officer but assured him that the matter would be taken care of. He left his name, address, and phone number so that the wrong could be made right after we had a little family council.

I was soon to turn five and was hoping desperately for a bicycle for my birthday. Needless to say, it was forfeited that year. The money my parents might have been saving for it went to buy a new windshield for the police officer.

*   *   *   *   *

As I was saying earlier, my childhood on the surface seemed normal enough, but emotionally I found myself a little troubled. I was almost 5-years-old and had developed a bed-wetting problem. My mother attempted to soothe my emotional distress by telling me that by the time I was five it would all be behind me.

The morning of my fifth birthday I awoke in a soaked bed and wet pajamas. Imagine my despair! I was now 5-years-old and had wet the bed—*on my birthday!* I was so disappointed, and more than that, I was terribly ashamed.

By my sixth birthday I had still not outgrown my problem, nor by the seventh, eighth, or ninth. No one could understand, especially not me. (In fact, when I was nine, my parents took me for a medical exam to see if something was wrong with my kidneys. I checked out all right, physically. So I was sent home without the mystery being solved or diagnosed).

I began to be the brunt of jokes by my siblings, and when

I started school, it wasn't long before the children at school also knew I had a problem. It seemed that the more distressed I became, the less control I had until I was having accidents sometimes even at school.

Daddy didn't understand either. His method of trying to handle the situation was to try to shame me. He seemed to think I was just being lazy about going to the bathroom; that somehow my bed-wetting was a choice I was making. It never crossed his mind, nor my own, nor anyone elses, that there might be some causative factor.

To be teased and made fun of by other children hurt me deeply. But when my own father did the same, I was more than hurt. I was traumatized. I felt that he did not understand me nor love me, that I did not please him, that I did not measure up, that he was ashamed of me.

The lack of understanding at home only served to aggravate my emotional and physical problems. The more I tried to overcome the wetting problem, the more of a problem the wetting became. I eventually resigned myself to the fact that I was just a wetter, and that I had no option but to live with the consequences.

* * * * *

To add to all my distress, thinking that I was abnormal, was the fact that from a very early age I found myself having romantic and even sexual fantasies—abnormal ones, toward men. My introduction to sexual behavior was by a young man, and it was perverted sexual behavior. And as that was all I had to relate to sexually, I found myself frequently reliving in my mind, the incident in the big farm truck under the tree. Perverted sexual fantasies seemed to have an ever increasing role in my thought processes from that age of four onward. Consequently, I felt very guilty but seemed to have no control over my thoughts. To some degree I feared men, and yet, at the same time had a strange attraction to them—a fascination that somehow did not seem to be normal. I longed for their approval and for their physical affection, and yet felt guilty for my longings. I was terribly confused by my emotions and feelings.

The bed wetting and the perverted sexual fantasies combined to make me believe that I was not like anyone else, that I truly was abnormal. I grew up with very low self-esteem, though most people would not have known it, because I excelled in my school work and did quite well in music. So, people thought I was "talented." Somehow, being musical was being "talented."

*   *   *   *   *

While I was still 5-years-old, we moved to another residential community in the city. It was there that I have my first recollections of music in our home. We had an old upright piano that Mamma got when she was 16-years-old. One day she was playing a little ditty to the delight of us children, and I remember being fascinated by my mother's fancy finger work. Eventually duty called in the kitchen, and she had to call it quits. She later told me that she was astonished to hear, coming from the living room, the same song being played back on the piano. Stepping back into the room to see what was going on, she found me playing the piano.

"That," said she, "was when I knew you needed to be taking piano lessons; you had an ear for and gift of music."

She made arrangements with a piano teacher who lived not too far away in the next community for both my brother and me, and thus began my music training. How I enjoyed taking piano lessons! My little mind was like a sponge soaking up everything the teacher could share with me. The daily practice periods were always enjoyable, for I thrilled to see my fingers learn to do what my ears heard my mother and teacher do on the piano. Mamma never had to encourage nor threaten in order to get me to practice, though she did have to get after my brother who never wanted to play in the first place. I always went beyond what was expected of me in practice time, for the piano became my new love interest.

My brother who hated piano practice, and the other boys, used to call me a "sissy," because often while they were outside "roughhousing," playing their games and sports, I was inside practicing the piano. I really enjoyed music, but it was also an escape for me.

* * * * *

My feeling of being unloved by my father was markedly reinforced on the occasion of my sixth birthday. I know now that he really did love me very much, but, like his own father, he was an incurable tease and had a very warped sense of humor at times. I was having a birthday party for the first time that I can remember. Maybe it's the only one I can remember because of his unique contribution. Little upside down ice cream cones were decorated to look like clowns. Mamma had a brand new lace table cloth being initiated at *my* birthday party. And there was actually a birthday cake in the middle of the table for me! All the family sat around the table and I was in the seat of honor.

"Why did some of them have that look of amused anticipation on their faces?" I wondered, but only for a fleeting second. This was all just too exciting!

Daddy reached over to light the six candles and then sat back. Something was strange about them. They sparkled and fizzed then *Bang! Bang! Bang!* They all blew up! And so did the cake! And one of the candles even burned a hole in Mamma's brand new lace table cloth.

As it turned out, to the knowledge of my brothers, Daddy had replaced the birthday candles with fire crackers! He and the boys really had a good laugh. It was a great practical joke!

Mamma cried. I cried. From then on I was frightened by firecrackers, guns, motorcycles, and cars with straight pipes; anything and everything that made loud noise. That made me less than a man-child in our family, because these were all the things that real men and boys truly appreciated. My older half-brother had come to live with us, and he was into all those things, which I reacted to with fear, if not abject terror. Along with my other unbecoming traits, I now had become the "Scaredy Cat."

It wasn't unusual for me to hear from the boys, "Ah! Go play with the girls!" So, I would. I always felt more comfort-

able, more at ease with, and more accepted by, the girls anyway. They weren't as rough and rowdy.

One entertainment the girls really enjoyed was dress up.
And I developed quite an affinity for it myself. In those days,
petticoats were in style. I can still remember, at seven years of
age, waltzing around the house to the amusement of my sisters,
but to the disgust of my brothers, with a petticoat on my head
for long, full hair, and one of my older sister's petticoats around
my waist making a stunning, floor length evening gown. (Perhaps this waltzing was a foreshadowing of sorts of what was
later to become a reality in my ballroom dancing instructor's
profession.)

Needless to say, I became increasingly alienated from the
family menfolk. As I became older, the gender gap seemed to
become ever wider between them and me.

Four

Childhood Paradise and Resentment

By the time I was 8-years-old, we had moved a couple more times and were now living outside a small country town in a big, white, two story plantation house that must have been 100-years-old. It was the main building on a large unused farm. This place was a paradise for children.

Besides the house, there was an old chicken house, a corn crib, a smoke house, a wood shed, another structure that could have been a servant's quarters, a barn, and an outhouse. The only plumbing inside the house itself was a kitchen sink.

My brother and I had the distinct privilege and responsibility of carrying out the slop jars, or honey buckets, to the outhouse every morning. This afforded us yet another opportunity to challenge one another as we discovered the scientific law of centrifugal force. We would sling the buckets around and around over our heads all the way across the yard and down the path, seeing who could make it without spilling the contents all over himself. It was great sport! One can see that we were very easily entertained!

The house itself had three attics, one of which we boys discovered through a secret door in our bedroom closet. Inside we found an old hand crank phonograph and stacks of old records, many of which were only one sided. We four children played them all, and they sounded so strange, like people singing through their noses and into tin cans or something. And the songs had such funny names, like "Fox Trot," whatever that meant.

We had many animals at this place—ducks, chickens, a turkey named "Stupid," a dog named Spot who could actually grin, and cats. Did we ever have cats! Every time Daddy came home from work, he complained that we seemed to have more cats. Well, we brought home every stray animal we could find, and they usually were cats. I lost count after we got to thirteen.

One day while playing out in the fields I caught a critter that seemed to have been injured somehow. It looked like its tail had been skinned. I brought it home, put Vaseline all over its tail and put it in a cage. Arriving home that evening and entering in through the back porch, Daddy saw the "pet" in the cage and called out to Mamma, "Honey, why do we have this rat in a cage on the back porch?" Well, needless to say, that pet didn't last too long!

We children hadn't much in the way of toys and electronic entertainment, and we didn't need it or miss it. We had the run of the woods and fields and found many ways to entertain ourselves.

Our neighbors were black. And, though we were born and raised in the south during the years of segregation, our mother taught us respect for our black neighbors and would never tolerate prejudice in her children in word or action. We made friends with these neighbor children who let us ride "Ol' Crow," their mule. We had fun visiting their little old run down shacks and playing with the little black children. But we were a bit scared off when they started killing their "pets" and butchering them. We were naive little vegetarians and were quite shocked to discover that some people actually ate their animals. Up until then, we had assumed all those cows, chickens, and pigs were play mates!

We had moved to this farm in the middle of the school year and were still going to church school in the big city about forty-five miles away. Our older half-sister was living with us at this time, and she drove Jake and me in to school every day in an old 1952 pink Nash. She was only fourteen herself and in the ninth grade. Mamma had to stay home with our little sisters who were not yet in school.

Our trips to and from school were always an adventure. Jeanie drove as if on the Daytona Speedway, and we would squeal with delight with her driving antics on the old back roads: squealing around sharp curves, hitting the high spots in the road fast enough to make us leave our seats, aiming for the largest water puddles to spray the water as far and wide as possible, and creating billowing clouds of dust on the dry dirt roads.

Frequently we stopped to pick up turtles along the road and take them to school in the big city to show off to all the city slicker boys and girls at school. Sometimes the turtles were big snapping turtles. They always caused quite a stir at school and made Jeanie quite a hit with the boys. Occasionally we would lose track of one of the turtles when we got home, but eventually, maybe even weeks later, Daddy followed his nose and found it decomposing under one of the car seats.

In spite of all the ways in which we could keep ourselves entertained and out of mischief on the farm, inevitably we ended up getting into some kind of trouble. One day Jake and I were summoned for disciplinary action, and on the way into the kitchen he stuck a magazine into his breeches. It looked like a great idea to me, so I did likewise. But mammas have a way of detecting these ploys, and, much to my dismay, for the first time ever she asked us to drop our drawers.

"Oh, no!" I thought. "This can't be happening to me!"

Jake reluctantly dropped his drawers, the magazine fell out, and he stood there in his underwear to get his spanking on the rear.

Putting on as stern a face as a softhearted mother could muster up, Mamma had to insist that I do the same. When I finally complied, my pants dropped down around my ankles, and my magazine also plopped out onto the floor. Only, to everyone's amazement, I stood there buck naked! Earlier I had had an accident, had taken off my shorts and left them who knows where and forgot about them. Now, not only was I being spanked for misbehaving, but my shameful wetting problem had once again been brought to attention. It seemed like I could never win!

When we first moved to the farm we had a television. My favorite show was *Zorro!* Zorro was my idol and became the subject of many of my perverted childhood romantic fantasies. I dreamed about riding with him as his sidekick. I imitated him in my behavior. I would try to dress up like Zorro, and even tried to get a Zorro costume one Halloween. I'm sure my parents were a little disturbed by my obsession with this television character, but they really had no idea how that show fed my perverted sexual appetite with food for my fantasies. How could they? I never talked to anyone about that dark, secret side of myself. I do know that I continued to grow increasingly frustrated with myself and more emotionally distressed with each passing year.

I found myself having ever more difficulty relating to boys because I could not seem to relate to their ideas of fun and games, especially competitive sports. I had a more gentle, tender, sensitive nature than most boys I knew. One incident that comes to mind that underscores this point was again between my brother Jake and me. We shared a second-story big bedroom with a ten foot ceiling. Every room in the house had a fire place, and our bedroom was no exception. In the spring when these fireplaces were not in use, the chimney swifts would build their nests in them. As the little ones hatched out, we could hear them way up inside the chimney peeping loudly at meal time as they competed for their food.

Jake, one day, became a bit annoyed at their ruckus and decided to put an end to it. He built a fire. I walked into the room and panicked in sympathy with the babies as I saw what he was doing. Running quickly downstairs, I committed the unpardonable sin; I tattled on him.

"Mamma! Come quick! Jake is murdering the babies in the chimney!" I yelled. "He's built a fire and is going to smoke them out!"

Mamma was the right one to go to. My tender heart was surpassed only by my mother's. Running upstairs with a pan of water, she quickly doused the fire and then summoned Jake for a little closed door session downstairs.

How I did not want to be labeled a tattle tale! But under the circumstances, the consequences never crossed my mind. Fortunately, I never heard another word about that incident from Jake, and don't remember ever being labeled a tattle tale.

Actually, Jake was really a neat brother most of the time. Being isolated out in the country as we were, we had to be civil to one another. We had very few playmates to choose from. I valued the time we were able to spend together for the most part, even though sibling rivalry did kick in upon occasion.

It was when other boys were around that problems usually developed between us. After all, how do you explain to the other boys why your brother still wets his pants at nine years of age? And that he'd rather play the piano than play base ball? Or, crochet?

"What?!"

"Well, yes!"

A little old lady friend of the family was very gifted at that delicate craft, and I was fascinated by it. So, she taught me how to crochet one summer. At nine years of age, I was crocheting doilies! And, I might add, was doing a fine job at it, much to the chagrin of my dad and the scorn and ridicule of my brother. I must confess, I really didn't make it very easy on the men folk in our family.

In addition to all my other peculiarities I added to their frustration in yet another way. Somehow I had developed a keen awareness regarding my personal appearance. While other boys ran around with hair cropped in crew cuts and flat tops, I was very meticulous about keeping my longer hair well combed with a perfect part over on the right side. A popular commercial jingle at the time was "Brylcreme, a little dab'll do ya." And I used my little dabs faithfully.

This was a constant irritation to my father who thought that I, a 9-year-old, spent entirely too much time on lookin' good. One day he was afforded the perfect opportunity to get this point across to me. He and my brother Jake had come across some hen eggs under a bush by the front steps to the big old house. Just about that time I came out of the house with every hair held in place by the "little dab'll do ya" Brylcreme.

That part in my hair was just too perfect. Without thinking it through carefully, or even at all, Daddy seized upon the opportunity and grabbed me playfully. Mind you, I know now he was not being mean. I know now that he loved me very much. But being the unmerciful tease that he was, and wanting to get me over my annoying habit of perfectionism in appearance, he cracked one of those fresh, raw eggs on my head and rubbed it into my hair, to the amusement of my brother.

Today we all can laugh about it together. But not that day, nor for years to come could I forgive and forget that humiliating ordeal. My efforts to gain approval, acceptance, and recognition only seemed to bring about disapproval, non-acceptance, ridicule, and scorn.

The battle over the hair issue only escalated. Daddy was our barber. One day in cutting our hair he cut Jake's first, giving him his usual flat top. Now, Jake could sport a flat top well. He had the perfect head for it. But I couldn't. Furthermore, I didn't like flat tops or crew cuts and was determined to not give in to that fad.

When my turn came to sit on the old barber stool, Daddy revved up the old clippers and then halted.

"Jesse [not my real name, but a nickname that had stuck with me since infancy], how do you want your hair cut this time?" he asked.

"Great!" I thought. "I still have some say so here."

"Just trim it around the edges" I replied.

At that point he took the clippers on a "close to the scalp" straight path down the middle of my head, from front to rear.

"Uh, How did you say you wanted it?" he asked, hardly able to contain his amusement.

It must have been an amusing sight to others. Here I sat with long hair sticking out either side of a reverse Mohawk, and nothing could be done but to finish it off with a crew cut! Once again, I was humiliated. The inevitable exclamations of those who saw me for the first time with this drastic change in my hair style would only serve to sink the knife deeper and to enlarge the open wound that could only partially heal with the slow growing out of my hair.

Daddy was surely unprepared for my reaction. I wilted in submission to my helplessness. In humiliation and resentment I withdrew further into myself emotionally, distancing myself from him. Again, he had not carefully thought out the consequences of his perverted sense of humor. To his credit, I must reveal that never again did he give me a crew cut or make such an issue out of the way I chose to wear my hair. I believe that he felt much remorse as he witnessed my pain and humiliation, though he tried to cover it up by laughing it off every time it came up.

Inside me, however, was simmering a caldron of resentment that would not be quenched for many years to come.

Five

Antics in the Attic
and Other Faux Pas

The forty-five mile trip to the city for school every day eventually became more of a challenge than our family could cope with, so the next school year we all went to public school. Realizing almost immediately that was a mistake, my parents decided to move closer to the city the following year so we could go back to church school. Our new home was still in the country, which we children really appreciated, and we remained there for the next four years.

Though at this point some might question, if not down right challenge, my perception, our childhood continued to be quite normal, as far as we could tell, and in many ways it was. For the most part, we children were quite content. Living in the country was so much more fun than living in the city.

In the previous home in the country, we all had learned to be quite the inquisitive explorers. We brought with us our curiosity which sometimes got us into trouble . . . In our snooping in this new house, we boys found the attic access in the ceiling of our bedroom closet. I don't know what it was about attics that fascinated us. But we really enjoyed playing in this one as we had in the other ones in the old farm house.

When my father discovered our antics in the attic, he forbade us to go up there any more. After all, the four of us ranged in age now from seven to eleven, and we were just too big to be up there horsing around.

One day Jake and my sisters decided to go up just one more time in direct disobedience to Daddy's instructions. At the risk of being labeled a "goody-goody," I refrained from going up at first. Then I began to worry. Suppose they were to get caught and get into trouble. I decided to go up and try to get them to come down. Using a stool to get up to the closet shelf, I pulled my way through the access hole and balanced myself on two adjacent ceiling joists. The ceiling was just drywall screwed to these beams. There was no insulation and no decking in the attic, so maneuvering up there was a real balancing act.

Shuffling along in the dim light with one foot on each timber, I called out to them in a loud whisper, "Hey, you guys! We're not supposed to be playing up here! Come on down before we all get caught!"

With much fuss they reluctantly complied and started for the access hole. I followed up in the rear. Being concerned about the ability of my younger sisters especially, I called out to them, again in a loud whisper, "Katie! Carol Lynn! Be careful! Don't slip, or you'll go right through the . . . Whoooaaah!"

Quick as a flash, before I knew it, my armpits were hanging on the joists, breaking my fall, sparing me from plunging into the room below. Hearing all the commotion, Mamma ran into her bedroom where, of course, Daddy slept as well, to see two legs kicking frantically through a hole in the ceiling right over the doorway into their bedroom at the foot of their bed. In shock, she watched as they wiggled their way back up through the black hole and disappeared.

"How could this have happened to me?" I said in anguish. I was trying to get them out of the attic so they wouldn't get in trouble! And now *I* had fallen through the ceiling! What would become of me now? My goose was surely cooked if ever any goose had been cooked before!

One by one, we four siblings plopped through the access hole in the closet and dropped to the floor below to meet the disapproving gaze of a mother in stunned disbelief. I explained what happened with the support of the others, and Mamma took on another attitude. We all were guilty of disobedience, but the one least guilty was the one who had fallen through. She seemed to be just as worried about the outcome of this mishap as I was.

Not knowing just what to do, right or wrong, she decided to patch the hole the best she could before Daddy got home. Finding a roll of scotch tape, she carefully stuck the hanging chunks of drywall back into place. It was a work of art, in my estimation, that took most of the role of tape to accomplish. But the hole was plugged, and maybe Daddy would not notice it.

The tactic worked. Daddy came home and never noticed the patched up hole in the ceiling. We all breathed a sigh of relief, because we knew that he would be furious if he discovered what we had done, what *I* had done.

Months later, Daddy walked into the room and happened to look up. By now, we had all forgotten about the accident and never paid attention to the patch work on the ceiling anymore.

"Marlene!" he called excitedly.

Mamma came into the room and found Daddy looking up at the brownish, brittle scotch tape curling away from the ceiling. Our secret was out, and Mamma was unmasked as an accomplice.

"What happened here? Who did this?"

Before the whole story could be told, my name was identified as the actual party who had crashed through the ceiling. Without hearing the rest of the story, my father grabbed me and threw me into my bedroom, slamming the door behind him. I had never seen Daddy in a rage like this before. And I was the object of his wrath. Pulling off his belt, he threw me against the wall. Then he began whipping me unmercifully and threw me against another wall. I was numb with fear, and to this day do not remember the pain of the whipping. Actually, I feared for my life. At this point my memory fails me. There is a blank spot there. I don't know how it all ended. I don't even remember if the ceiling ever got repaired. I do know that although I survived the punishment physically, emotionally I was a wreck. I now feared my father more than ever, and my anger and resentment toward him only deepened.

What was the use? Here I was 10-years-old and still unable to avoid bringing him to wrath. All the other phobias were only magnified, and within me boiled that caldron of resentment and anger that I did not know how to deal with. So I suppressed it. The festering of something really ugly was growing inside me.

*   *   *   *   *

Needless to say, my bed-wetting problem was still with me. But I found a solution to that vexation. Up until now I had been sharing a bedroom with my brother Jake, and we both had slept in the same bed. So, whenever I wet the bed at night, I sometimes wet him too. That, of course, did not work to enhance our relationship! On one rare occasion when we had the chance to sleep in separate beds, he actually wet the bed himself, the one and only time in his life, and had the gall to blame me; as if I would actually crawl into his bed, relieve myself, and then return to my own! Honestly! But he seriously believed that somehow I had done it!

On the back of the house was a closed in porch that Mamma had been using for storage. I asked if I could move into it if I cleaned it up and organized it, and she gave me permission. After years of being in storage, much of the stuff was totally ruined and irredeemable. So, I threw it out. What was good, I boxed up on one wall, covered it real neatly with a bed spread and moved in.

In the stuff, I found a complete set of bed linens, green with white ruffled trim, and there were curtains to match; enough to dress all seven windows on the two outside walls. In this room, I discovered my own obsession with neatness and orderliness. My room was my private sanctuary. No one was allowed entrance except on rare occasions. My made up bed was off limits. I would not allow one wrinkle anywhere. I felt safe in that room.

*   *   *   *   *

To avoid detection and ridicule as much as possible, I became very skillful at covering up my bed-wetting problem, or so I thought. At the age of ten, I began stripping down my bed in the middle of the night and hiding the evidence. Then, when no one was around, I would do the laundry. While appearing to be very helpful around the house doing this type of chore (to my mother's delight), I was really just making a desperate attempt to protect myself from scoldings, taunts, and ridicule.

In this little country home we had an old ringer washer. Mamma was taking nursing, and we children were left at home under teenage supervision one summer. Running sheets through the ringer was really tricky business for a kid. Not knowing any better, I would start by putting one corner of the sheet into the ringer. By the time the sheet got half way through it was quite bulky and needed a lot of assistance in order not to jam the rollers. It was not uncommon at that point to get my fingers caught in the ringer, and it would start eating me up! With a little quick action on my part, I could bang the release with my other hand and get free.

One day my grandmother was staying with us while our parents were both at work. I was doing laundry. I did lots of laundry in those days. When I pulled out a sheet to run it through the ringer, all was going well until it came to the middle bulky portion. As usual, I was very deftly working to keep the bulk evenly spread on the rollers when, all of a sudden, they grabbed my fingers and in I went. In panic, I started yelling, kicking, and banging on the release with my free hand, but it would not release. Before I knew it, the ringer had eaten my arm all the way up to the elbow, where it jammed and wouldn't go any further.

With my free hand I stopped the machine, but my arm was still locked in the ringer. I called frantically to my grandmother, "Help! Help! I'm caught in the ringer!"

She came running in, all frantic. "Land sakes alive, Jesse! How did you get all caught up in that thing?"

Granny banged and banged on the release herself, but to no avail. In a panic herself, she finally ran next door to the little country store to get help. It seemed like she was gone forever, and here I was stuck up to my elbow in an old ringer washer. Eventually she returned with Miss Mabel from the store, and the two of them were able to get me free.

Some time later, my little sister, Carol Lynn, who was no more than eight, was trying her hand at doing the laundry. You guessed it! I heard her crying out for help from the other room. Running in, I found her with her arm up to the elbow in the old ringer washer. I tried the release. Nothing happened. She was frantically crying out for me to do something. I had to think quick. Nothing was working. Then I had a bright idea. Why hadn't I thought of it before when this happened to me? I put the ringer in reverse and ran her arm back through. As her fingers popped out from between the rollers I was so proud of myself. But when Mamma got home I got a real scolding. At the end of each finger was a humdinger of a blood blister! Evidently, reverse was not the best way to escape the jaws of the old ringer washer.

I believed that by becoming so helpful in doing laundry that I had skillfully succeeded in covering up my bed-wetting problem, thus avoiding detection and ridicule. Was I ever mistaken!

My twelfth birthday was another memorable one for me, though a party was not in the plans. Since my birthday is only two days before Christmas, I sometimes felt cheated. My parents would hide my present under the Christmas tree. When it was brought out and given to me, I always suspected they were giving me one of my Christmas presents for a birthday present and that I wasn't really getting a birthday present at all. In fact, on Christmas morning, I even imagined, selfishly, that I was short changed in Christmas presents.

Anyway, on this birthday the family was all sitting around the living room in my honor. They sang the usual "Happy Birthday to you." Then my father passed around my birthday card for everyone else to see first. The sibling glee made me a bit uneasy.

When the card came to me, I gazed at it in stunned disbelief! It was for a 1-year-old! The picture was of a toddler in a diaper riding a broom stick horse. Penciled in were drops of "water" dripping from the diaper and a puddle on the floor under the baby's feet. "Happy Birthday!"

If the floor could have opened and swallowed me up, I would have been grateful. How could my own father humiliate me so, and in front of the whole family? The rest of the evening is mercifully gone from my memory.

*   *   *   *   *

On a lighter note, it was at this age of twelve that I received my last whipping from my mother. Jake and I had gotten into a scuffle, and I was chasing him around the house. Being twelve and thirteen, we were much too big to be running in the house, and, besides, it had always been against the rules.

"Boys, quit running in the house!" Mamma warned.

Well, Jake wasn't going to quit running and let me catch him. And I wasn't going to stop running until he did stop so that I could catch him.

"Boys!" Mamma called out a little louder. "I said to stop running in this house."

"I can't," Jake called back on the run. "Jesse's chasing me!"

"Well, if he'd stop running away I could stop chasing him." I added breathlessly, whizzing past Mamma.

"Jesse," Mom called out. "Stop chasing your brother!"

"Make *him* stop first," I shot back.

On this pass through, Mamma caught my arm, bringing to a halt the great chase. She then asked for my belt.

"But, Mamma!" I whined, reluctantly pulling off my brand new Indian bead belt and handing it to her. As I looked her in the face, I started to giggle. She was a bit exasperated. Her face flushed red, her mouth was tense with determination, and I could see fire in her eyes. This was so rare to see in my gentle, easily manipulated mother, that somehow I just found it humorous.

She doubled up the belt and gave me a lick with it.

"Ow!" I yelped. But I couldn't stop laughing; she looked so funny. Of course, Jake thought it was all pretty comical, too. The more I laughed, the more Mamma applied the belt. I dropped to the floor and started rolling around to dodge the belt. This had become a game to me.

"Jesse, hold still, and stop laughing!" she demanded struggling not to laugh herself.

"Mamma, you look so funny when you're mad!" I laughed more.

"Jesse," she ordered. "Stop rolling around and take your punishment!" She was now breaking up into a little laughter herself.

The belt was hitting the floor more than my derriere, and the Indian beads started popping off the belt and flying around the room. I could not regain my composure, and Mom could not retain her own. At that point, the episode came to a conclusion as we all three laughed together about the whole ridiculous scene. Jake and I had totally forgotten the reason for our scuffle.

She later told me that she knew my whippin' days were over when the generated response was laughter. I should have thought of that myself, years earlier!

Six

Nightmare of All Nightmares

A year had passed since my humiliating twelfth birthday. At that time, I couldn't imagine anything worse ever happening to me. But I was soon to discover that things could be and would be worse.

The competition experienced between Jake and myself, I must acknowledge, was mostly on my part since I was the younger and was more desperate to achieve and even excel. In school, Jake never really had to crack a book. He was just naturally smart with an IQ of 135. If he wanted to, he could make straight *A*s just by being present in class. It seemed that he just soaked in information naturally. I, on the other hand, had to work harder at it. Being at the top of my class was important to me; it was a goal I always maintained and usually achieved.

Our little school was small enough that each teacher and classroom had two grades. So, every other year, Jake and I were in the same room. This was one of those years; he in the eighth grade and I was in the seventh. Though very timid, especially when in the lower grade in the classroom, I nevertheless always enjoyed being in the same classroom with my brother, because I believed myself to be more in his peer group those years.

Growing up, I always felt unequal to Jake who was very popular in school, excelled in sports, and always had the girls chasing after him. This was accentuated at times when I felt put down by him, like the night we slept over with the two sons of our teacher. At bed time, Jake started joking about not letting me sleep on the top bunk if they didn't want to get "rained on" during the night. He really meant no harm and was just having fun at my expense. However, this was very embarrassing to me. He and I ended up sleeping on the floor in sleeping bags. And, wouldn't you know it, that was one of those nights when I lost control. Mortified and in a panic, I just rolled up the sleeping bag and pretended nothing had happened. (I often wondered whatever they must have thought weeks later when they opened it up for their own personal use).

Anyway, not having a change of clothes, I ended up putting my pants on over my wet shorts, only to end up at school with wet pants, too! It was very challenging for me to keep myself hidden in my desk long enough to dry out so as to go undetected. But that incident pales in significance with what was yet to come.

One day the nightmare of all nightmares happened to me in school that scarred me for many years to come. It was getting fairly close to recess time, and I had to go to the restroom. In order to get permission, a student would have to raise a hand with one finger, so the teacher would know the situation and could nod approval.

For some reason, I decided to wait until recess, though my need to go was increasingly urgent. I was too embarrassed to raise my hand so that all could see that I needed to go. And before I knew it, I had wet my pants, just a little. But it was enough to show, and I panicked.

"What will everybody think?" I just couldn't bear the thoughts of all those students snickering at me when they discovered that I had lost control. So I labored intensely to maintain control and to make it to recess. But I couldn't. Pretty soon I wet a little more, and a little more. Then, in disgrace, I buried my head in my arms on the desk as inevitably I relieved myself completely.

Pretty soon someone noticed this ever widening puddle of water around my desk and got the attention of the teacher. He came to me and quietly asked if I were all right. Without looking up, I shook my head.

"Are you sick?" he asked kindly.

I nodded my head, again without looking up.

No one snickered, at least within my hearing. And the teacher dismissed the class for recess. He then told me that he would call home for me. While no one was in the class room, I went to the rest room preparing to stay there for the rest of the day until someone came to take me home. The door opened, and in walked *my dad,* the last person in the world I wanted to see at a time like this. He had a change of clothes, and, surprisingly, he looked upon me with pity. But I couldn't look at him. I just hung my head in shame.

"You know?" he said in an effort to console me, "Once, when I was in third grade, I did the same thing."

Shocked by this new revelation, I almost felt better. "But I'm in the seventh grade!" I sulked.

"There was another time when I had an even more embarrassing experience," he continued.

At first hesitating, he then proceeded to tell me about an experience in fourth grade, having to sit on the front row, and struggling with a very bad case of "effluvium." Unable to contain himself, he had become the unwilling source of entertainment for his classroom as he unavoidably released a long series of outbursts that whistled because he was straining so hard to keep it under control.

"You've got to be kidding!" I retorted with amazed amusement.

"Honest Injun," he chuckled, looking off into the distance as if revisiting the scene of his own humiliation.

Pretty soon Dad had me laughing in spite of myself. Now I understood the origin of one of Grandpa's pet nicknames for us children—"Whistle Britches!" It must surely have been first assigned to my father when he himself was a little boy.

I changed clothes, but he did not take me home. Wisely, he had me go on to the next class, which happened to be choir practice. No one was unkind to me, though they all knew what had happened. School went on, but the humiliation I had brought upon myself lingered for years. However, in later years

the memory of dad sharing with me his own schoolroom humiliation in an effort to console me in my day of disgrace
served to ease the tension between us, helping to pave the way
for our reconciliation.

Seven

On the Brighter Side

Have I already mentioned that on the surface my childhood seemed normal enough? Lest the wrong impression be given by the enumeration of negative experiences in my childhood, I must say that there were many happy experiences I could elaborate upon: like Dad teaching us boys how to drive trucks and tractors when we were nine and ten-years-old; raising our own farm animals—cows, horses, chickens, ducks, turkeys, dogs and cats, pigeons, guinea pigs, mice, Jo-Jo our crow, Coony our raccoon; swinging on grapevines in the woods (and even smoking a little grapevine now and then . . .); exploring the fields and the forests; swimming in the country creeks and mud holes; plopping down in a clump of honey suckle to savor the delicate sweetness of the nectar, until some busy bee decided to unseat us; playing on the cotton bales at night when the cotton gin was closed; climbing trees when we were supposed to be chopping cotton.

But the focus of my story is to examine factors that no doubt played a part in my becoming homosexual as I matured into manhood; therefore the enumeration of experiences that are mostly unpleasant to my memory.

In defense of my brother Jake, however, I must share one incident that portrays the kind of decent and noble person he really was, and yet is to this day.

One day we were in the cotton patch in the back forty at my grandparents farm and were supposed to be chopping cotton. Our hoes had been freshly filed to almost razor sharp. It was the middle of the day and we were tired of chopping those

57

seemingly endless rows. One of us . . . picked up a mud clod and tossed it at the other and scored a hit. Well, that little act of aggression, of course, had to be returned. Almost immediately the fun escalated into an all out mud ball fight. Jake was older and bigger and stronger, and I soon found myself in swift retreat, only to discover him to be in hot pursuit. Dragging my hoe behind me, I shifted into high gear. My razor sharp hoe hit a clod, bounced up, and chopped down on the back of my ankle leaving a three inch long gaping slash. I panicked at the sight of my own gushing blood. But Jake, catching up to me quickly tore a rag off something and tied it tightly around my ankle. Then picking me up (and I was almost as big as he was at the time), he carried me all the way from the back forty to grandpa's house where I was quickly driven to the doctor to be stitched back together.

Jake was my hero. He really cared for me. And "where the rubber met the road," he demonstrated his brotherly love and decency. Yes, we were involved in sibling rivalry, and that was not to cease. But the older we got, the better friends we became.

I'll never forget the day when a bunch of us country kids lined up on the road in front of our house for a race. Dad did the countdown, "Ready, Set . . . Go!" And we were off. I ran for all I was worth. If only I could win, or at least come in ahead of my brother. Maybe I could have a little respect from all these kids. With a determination I didn't know I could muster, I edged him out for first place! Though defeated by his kid brother, Jake actually seemed to be a little proud. That has remained a treasured moment in the annals of my mind. And Dad was proud, too!

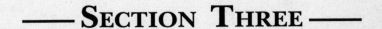

—— SECTION THREE ——

Those Troubled Teen Years

Eight

Loss of
Innocence; . . . Again!

Entering my early teens, I remember *National Geographic* being one of my favorite magazines. I'm sure my parents were pleased with my interest, because it was known to be very educational. One of my uncles had collected these magazines for years, and whenever we went to visit him I thoroughly enjoyed browsing through them. But what I enjoyed looking at most were such things as the artists depictions of cave man society with all its raw, naked strength graphically portrayed. The articles and the photography of naked natives and aborigines in primitive places also fascinated me, as did the pictures of scuba divers in their sea world, athletes in motion, and any pictures that revealed the bodies of healthy men.

Another source of learning I much enjoyed was encyclopedias. In them I came across all sorts of photographs of nude statuary representing the Greek gods and heroes of antiquity, and the artwork of Michelangelo. The women figures always looked rather plump, small breasted and unattractive. However, the male objects were always very muscular, rugged and sensual. They captivated my imagination and were likewise a great source of inspiration for me.

Actually, it seemed that any illustrations that showed partially clothed, tightly clothed, or naked humanity; whether in art, dance, (especially ballet), science, or sports; all had served to arouse my mental sexual appetite and to feed my ever growing fantasies.

Summer boys' camps were an eye opener to me. One year I shared a cabin with some boys who openly practiced masturbation. Their behavior was disgusting to me at the time but served to further my education in perverted sexual behavior nevertheless.

On the other hand, camp had afforded me opportunities to interact with objects of my growing lust for men. As a child, I virtually fell in love with many of the camp counselors and staff who were high school and college students. They were very athletic, outgoing, fun-loving and downright beautiful in their swimsuits and casual camp attire. I took advantage of all the water activities; taking swimming lessons, ski lessons, and canoeing; thoroughly enjoying association and physical contact with these men. As counselors, they showed us boys much personal attention, which I would later fantasize into affection and intimacy.

My attractions to men intensified with time and with indulgence. One day I was picked up and given a ride into town by the new service station attendant. He looked like one of those Greek gods with his dark brown hair, perfectly chiseled manly features, V-shaped torso, and massive muscles accentuated by tight-fitting tee shirt and blue jeans. I couldn't believe the feelings that swept over me being alone in the car with this man.

Next door to the service station lived close friends of our family. Their daughter was in my grade at school, and she was love sick over this same man. Sometimes, while our family visited them at night, when no one was watching, she and I would peek through the curtains and watch this man's every move. I would tease her and egg her on and get just as much enjoyment out of watching him as she did.

In a magazine one day, I noticed an add for a Charles Atlas home course in body-building. The picture of the muscle bound man in his swim suit inspired me to invest in my own self-improvement. I had this notion that if I looked like this man, then I would be better accepted in the world of men from which I felt so distant. When the packet arrived, I had hoped to be able to retrieve it and secret it away in my bedroom. However, I was not the one to bring in the mail that day, and my ambition to become the next Atlas became the subject of much jesting and derision. After all, I was all of 12-years-old at that time, slim of build, and not interested in competitive sports. The picture of a piano playing, crocheting, bed-wetting body builder was justifiably laughable, I must admit.

At the age of thirteen and in the eighth grade I was one of the boys who blossomed a little more slowly into puberty than some of the others. This was realized to be to my advantage in some ways. In the school choir, I was singing alto along with the girls. Because of my gift at harmonizing, I was one of four boys singled out to start a gospel quartet. I would sing first tenor since my voice had not yet changed. The other three boys were fifteen and in the ninth grade, and they sang the other three parts.

We became quite good very quickly and soon we were singing for special music at churches and revival meetings and other special functions on the weekends. Being that I lived outside the city some distance into the country, it was difficult for my parents to get me to some of these functions. So, one of the boys invited me to spend these weekends at his home. It seemed to be the perfect solution. After all, not only were we both in the quartet, we were also becoming good friends.

After school on those particular Fridays, Danny and I would be at his home alone for several hours before his working parents got home. It was on these occasions that Danny took me into his parents' bedroom, sneaked into one of their dresser drawers and pulled out a book (perfectly kosher for adults, I'm sure), on the reproductive system and sexual intercourse. It was complete with illustrations the likes of which my virgin eyes had never seen. Yes, I had seen other sexually stimulating photographs and works of art, but nothing as explicit as this!

As Danny and I looked through this book, he got all excited about these pictures and then started telling me his fantasies about feeling and touching one of the girls back at school. One day he got so excited that he, to my surprise, started play acting some of his feeling/touching fantasies on me. I didn't quite know what to do. He was very persistent. He was older. He was a friend. He told me not to worry, that he did the same with one of the other boys in my class. I suppose that meant it was normal and acceptable behavior.

I was so vulnerable and so easily intimidated for some reason that I did not know how to resist, even though I felt very awkward and ill at ease. To me this was sinful, yet I seemed to be totally helpless to resist these awkward situations. I did nothing to encourage him, but remained a rigid and passive party to his play acting. But my passive toleration served only to encourage him further.

These repeated episodes of uninvited advances, experimentation, and exploration into the world of sexuality, escalated to the point of getting totally out of hand, and, once introduced, I then fell into the shameful practice of occasional self-abuse when I was alone at home. The feelings of guilt that flooded over me on those occasions were almost overwhelming, and I would *promise* God that I would never, never do it again. My covenant with the Lord was no better than that old covenant of ancient Israel. I would hold out for a long time, but eventually I would have another, and yet another moral fall.

This was a major turning point in my life. Up until this time, all my sexual behavior had been purely mental. Now I had become sexually active! What was to one teen age boy just experimentation and play that never diminished his attraction to the opposite sex, was to me a source of confusion and a reinforcement in the direction I was unknowingly headed. While he fantasized about some girl, I usually fantasized about some particular boy or man during my episodes of self-abuse.

Outwardly, I appeared to be a normal, happy, Christian young man. Indeed, I was quite conscientious about all my Christian beliefs and standards that could be demonstrated outwardly. In actuality, I was a little hypocrite. My desire for acceptance, approval and excellence never waned, but only grew with my physical maturity and with my feelings of ever increasing secret moral failure.

*   *   *   *   *

Parents, summer camp staff, school faculty and staff, etc., take note and beware: unsupervised "sleep overs" at home, school, camp, and other outings; and open communal showers for boys in schools and camps, all provide opportunities for improper education of your children and for temptation they may not be ready to face.

Nine

Excellence in Achievement and Confusion of Heart

Toward the end of eighth grade in school, my teacher came to me and asked me to write a speech for graduation. I was the valedictorian! This was a monumental achievement for me. I enjoyed school and always studied hard to make good grades. Quizzes and tests were not something I dreaded, but, rather, something that gave me opportunities to be recognized for excellence. Quite often recognition for high scores was given publicly, and this fed my need, actually my desire, for approval and acceptance.

When the excitement of being asked to give a speech for graduation wore off, it suddenly dawned on me that I had never written a speech before, nor given one. Besides that, I was very timid and had suffered episodes of stage fright in the past. Like, the first time I had attempted playing the piano publicly; for the theme song at a tent revival. About halfway through the song I missed a chord, the congregation got a beat ahead of me, and I froze. Being only about 10-years-old, I was so embarrassed that I fled the tent and hid in the family truck until the meeting was over and we went home.

Later, at a piano recital at school I was playing the "Ben Hur Chariot Race March." This recital had been well advertised among our family and church, so *everybody* was there. During the *finale*, I lost my place. Thinking quickly on my seat, I just went back to the beginning of the *finale* and played it again. When I reached the difficult area once more, the same

thing happened. I ended up going round and around several
times before I could successfully get to the final chord, which
I struck with all the display of confidence I could fake. One of
my older cousins in the back of the audience remarked to my
mother, "My! I can't believe they gave Jesse such a long number to play on his first recital! I thought he'd never get to the
end!" Mom, however, being familiar with the piece of music,
knew the truth; that I was surely having a panic attack up there
trying to bring Ben Hur triumphantly across that finish line.

The memory of my history of embarrassing experiences at
public events caused me to recoil at the thought of now having
to give a valedictorian speech. I had earned the opportunity,
but now wished I hadn't.

The little lady who taught me how to crochet years earlier
was a godly Christian lady whom I really admired. Not knowing how to write a speech, I went to her for assistance. She
wrote out what appeared to me a masterpiece of oratory. Of
course, it was meant to be a guideline from which I could draw
some ideas and to which I could add some of my own. I
studied it, and studied it some more. There was no room for
improvement whatsoever. So, on the night of graduation I read
it word for word with all the pride of ownership the President
of the United States has when reading his "own" speeches.

During the ensuing summer, we moved away to a college
in another state where Dad had been hired to run the dairy for
the agriculture department. Jake and I were enrolled in the
ninth and tenth grades; Katie and Carol Lynn in the sixth and
seventh grades.

The world of high school was worlds apart from elemen-
tary school. The college afforded all kinds of opportunities for
students who wanted or needed to work their way through
school. That summer before school started, I was hired to work
on the farm. Since I already knew how to drive tractors, it
wasn't long before I was allowed to cultivate the fields and
operate various kinds of farm equipment. I was assigned to
work with one fellow who was a senior in academy and, in my
estimation, was a real bully. Bossy and insensitive, I took an
instant dislike to him. One of our assignments was to pull

silage off the wagon onto a conveyor belt that fed it into a blower that would shoot it up into the silo. Silage is foul smelling stuff. It's a bit like sauerkraut for cows and smells putrid as it ripens in a silo.

Usually, my job was to be up in the silo with a pitchfork spreading the silage around so it would fill the silo evenly. The one below would have to mix a white powdered preservative with the silage as it was being dumped on the conveyor belt. Billy was not considerate of me up in the silo. He would dump little bits in sporadically, and little poofs of this powder would blow into the silo. Highly irritating to my nose, it would cause me to have sneezing fits and virtually disable me at my job. No matter how I implored him to be more careful, he seemed totally careless of my well-being.

After lunch one day, we swapped jobs, he thinking, I suppose, that my job up in the silo was easier than his at the wagon. Now was my chance to get even! The "ornery little cuss" in me became irrepressible. I worked for a little while pulling off the silage and sprinkling the preservative just right, keeping a constant flow on the conveyor belt so as not to give him any rest up there in the silo. Then I poured straight powder on the belt and watched it poof out each joint of the shoot on its way up. Suddenly it hit the top. But by now I was innocently and diligently feeding pure silage onto the belt, and lots of it. Looking up I saw white powder billowing out the top of the silo, and two arms flailing frantically out the opening.

"Stop! Stop!" Billy yelled, coughing and choking. "Hey! Stop! You're killing me up here!"

From that day on, we had a healthy respect for one another mingled with a little mutual disdain.

When summer ended and school started, I was rotated to another job, campus mail boy. I really enjoyed that opportunity to get to know just about everyone on campus in the Academy as well as the College and the various industries. By the second semester, I had acquired an even better job working at the campus grocery store.

Working was always enjoyable for me. It instilled in me an appreciation for my education, as I was working so hard to pay

for it. In school, I excelled. To my amazement, I was elected
to be freshman class president. Jake was elected by his class as
president also. We both were doing quite well in school, actually.

In one of my more normal phases, I developed a little
crush on one of the girls in my freshman class. She was very
nice to me and friendly, but didn't seem to reciprocate my
interest as I had hoped. Then I discovered that she had her
eyes on my brother! In fact, they even dated for awhile. Boy!
Did that knock some props out from under me!

My sister Katie brought some of her girl friends home and
introduced them to Jake and me. They were in seventh and
eighth grade, however, too young for us high school boys. But
they were quite cute and nice, and so we both developed an
interest. However, when we were together, both girls vied for
the attention of my brother, and I felt like a fifth wheel.

Katie brought around a couple more of her friends later,
one of whom actually liked me, and me alone. We developed
a little teenage romance that consisted of going to lyceums
together and church sometimes and just walking together publicly on campus. It was all very innocent, and fortunately so for
me, because while enjoying her friendship and the masquerade
of having a normal boy/girl relationship, I found myself being
secretly more attracted to a couple of the upperclass jocks and
some of the college boys.

Being a Christian, I was quite disturbed by these fascina-
tions, but felt powerless to stop them. Outwardly, I was achiev-
ing a little popularity in school; being well liked and highly
thought of by faculty, staff, and students on campus; maintaining a "courtship" with a girl, and a very pretty one at that. Yet
inside, I was suffering unexplainable confusion and turmoil.
What could I possibly do about my unnatural romantic and
even sexual fantasies toward these boys on campus? What would
my girlfriend think if she knew of my mental struggle between
her and them?

I worked hard, I studied hard, and I practiced hard at my
music. I remember a group of girls hanging around outside the
window one day where I was taking my piano lesson. "Oh!

Listen to Jesse play that piano! Isn't he talented?" they giggled. "Is that what he's going to play for the recital?" they asked my teacher.

"Yes!" she replied. "What do you think of it?"

"It's great!" And they hurried off to their after-school activities.

As the piano recital approached, I was practicing one day in the auditorium. I didn't know it at the time, but my brother Jake and my mother were listening. "Mom," Jake said. "He really is good, isn't he?" It was twenty-five years later that Mom thought to reveal that observation to me. And I mused, "If only I had known then that he respected my musical skill and ability! I had ceased caring what his opinion about it was by that time, so I imagined. But when she shared with me his comment, I realized how much his opinion really did mean to me. Twenty-five years late, but still, it really touched my heart.

During that school year, a group of students were selected to go to another boarding academy for a Bible conference. Jake and I both were included. I was assigned to room with a dorm student at this school, likewise a freshman, who obviously was a conscientious, ambitious Christian student. He was such a nice young man; clean cut, handsome, and obviously spending time in the gym working out. We became instant friends and even pen pals. But I never felt quite sure about my feelings toward him. He was just the kind of person I always wanted as a close friend, but my unnatural feelings left me feeling unworthy of such a friend.

Throughout my highschool years, this turmoil only grew, as I constantly had to wrestle with my feelings, trying to sort out the good ones from the bad ones. It was very difficult for me to separate these feelings. If I liked someone as a friend, I felt guilty for my attraction, because I associated attractions with my fantasies, and my fantasies were naughty. So, having boys as friends was not easy for me, even though I very much wanted them. What confusion of heart!

Ten

On My Own, Away from Home, and a Broken Heart

At the age of fifteen, I heard about a little private boarding school where everyone studied music of one kind or another. Being in the same school with my very popular brother had been a real challenge for me, though I loved him very much. As we got older we became better and better friends. Yet we drifted apart as we attempted to excel in totally different areas, he in sports and with girls, and I with scholastics and music. While he was rather skilled socially, I was still quite uneasy and unsure of myself. The girls that I liked quite often seemed to be totally disinterested in me once they met my handsome, athletic brother.

It would be very exciting, I thought, to go away to school where no one knew me; where no one knew of my embarrassing problem; where I could pretend to be just as normal as everyone else; where I could have a brand new start at life.

The school was very exclusive, and I could think of no one to use for a reference. But to my amazement and delight I was accepted for my sophomore year. One of the members of our church drove me the two hundred miles to the school at the beginning of the summer and left me on the front porch of the boys dormitory. What a feeling! I was now on my own and away from home!

The school operated on a work/study plan, and by working there full time all summer, enough of my tuition would be worked off that my parents could then afford to pay the remainder on a monthly basis.

Though no one seemed to be expecting me when I arrived, they soon put me to work anyway. My summer was very full, and I became friends with the other students who were working the summer program as well. In fact, I found myself to be very well accepted and almost popular at this new school. What a break!

Shortly before school started that fall, my parents came up for a visit and brought Katie and Carol Lynn with them. My brother had decided to go off to another boarding academy in another state. My sisters brought with them one of their friends, a tall, thin girl with an olive complexion, and long, straight, dark hair. She was introduced to me as Rachel, and she just stood there with her hands clasped behind her back, twisting from side to side with the biggest grin on her face. Actually, it was quite a pretty grin. But, if she was a friend of Katie's, then she couldn't be a girl friend of mine! I was fifteen now. She was only thirteen, and Katie tended to meddle too much in my dating affairs and usually caused a disaster: like the time she invited one of her friends to be my date to the fair when I had already asked another girl that I was somewhat interested in. So, at the naive age of thirteen, I ended up with two girls on my first date, not knowing what to do with either one of them! And they didn't get along with each other at all.

A few weeks later when school started, Rachel came as a freshman student. Her brother was there as a junior, and I was a sophomore. We soon became very good friends, but that was it. But it was one of those friendships that sticks for life; that meant a lot to me, especially in later years.

I had been at the boarding school for several months before I realized that my trouble with incontinence had totally disappeared! Out from under the disapproval I felt at home over this impediment, I suddenly no longer had the problem! To me, this was a major achievement in my growing up. Ten years late, for I had aimed at outgrowing this by age five, nevertheless I had finally surmounted the insurmountable. Wow! What freedom! What release I felt!

I spent three years at this academy and loved it. Here I studied piano with the best instructor I had ever met. A professional accompanist, she not only advanced my piano skills, but also taught me to play church organ as well.

What I really wanted more than anything, though, was to be able to sing. My youngest sister, Carol Lynn, later joined me at this academy, took up voice lessons and excelled. How I wanted to be able to sing, too! We did have much fun with music together, however. I became her accompanist, and some of our mutual best memories are of our joint interest in music and being able to perform together.

My singing ambitions and career, however, came to an abrupt halt that very first year. The voice teacher was quite elderly. In her younger years she had been a radio singer, and her 14-year-old daughter (now my piano teacher), had been her accompanist. Somehow, in her old age she had lost sensitivity to the acute awareness of young teenage boys to the opinions of their peers. A recital was coming up, and she selected a song for me to sing. When I saw the name of the song and read the lyrics, I recoiled in horror! How could anyone ask a 16-year-old boy to sing this little child's song?

All my pleadings for a change of song fell on deaf ears. No! This was the one that had to be sung. I had nightmares worrying about getting up in front of that school to perform those childish lyrics.

The unavoidable day inevitably came. To my dismay, my family showed up. My sister Katie, always quick to poke fun, snicker, and tease at others' misfortunes, was sitting on the back row. I felt like Charlie Brown of the "Peanuts" cartoon facing the inevitable condescension of Lucy.

"Oh! How could I get up and make such a total fool out of myself?"

I can still remember that look of malicious glee on Katie's face as I belted out the lyrics, ". . . But the Big Brown Bear Goes 'Woof!'" I knew that I could never live that one down. She had "food for fodder" for years to come, and she used it, too!

So ended my singing ambitions and career. I remained in the school choir. It was mandatory. But I dropped the voice lessons for good.

The work/study program at this school was terrific. We all worked half a day during the school year and had classes the other half. Class work kept us so busy, and work kept us so tired that most of us had no time to even think about getting into trouble.

Operating on a self-supporting basis, the school had its own farm, garden, dairy, and sanitarium. The students helped build the faculty homes, the church building, the dormitories, the swimming pool, assisted in mechanics, and kept the school warm in winter by shoveling coal in the boiler room. We raised most of our own food, harvested it, and canned or froze it for the coming year. The girls worked as nurses aides in the sanitarium, cooks in the cafeteria and sanitarium, or worked in the campus laundry. The educational focus of the school was to develop a balance of the spiritual, mental, and physical faculties of its students. As stated above, some of the best years and best memories of my life centered around my three years at this school.

This environment was not, however, successful in totally distracting me from what was festering inside. Somehow I got hold of some Tarzan novels. Reading these books opened a door to fantasy land that I had never ventured into before. As with the Zorro character idolized in my childhood, I now became obsessed with the fictional character of Tarzan, imagining looking like him, being like him, and living like he did. Reading these novels really worked to add to my confusion. Sometimes I identified with the Jane character, and sometimes with Tarzan. But most of all, I fantasized about being with him, being the focus of his heroic exploits, his attentions and affections. The Jane character needed to go. It was under this kind of inspiration that I began seriously working on my own physique. Tarzan was my new hero, my idol; I began pumping iron.

The boys on campus were nice and fun to be around in school, in work, and in play. One of the upper class boys that I really looked up to had a sister in the freshman class. He liked me and encouraged me to develop an interest in his sister, which I did. She responded favorably, and soon we were carrying on a secret courtship by letters, for we were not allowed to pair off in this school, but were expected instead to develop our social skills by being friends with everyone. This was a good policy in theory, but difficult to practice as well as to enforce.

On one of the holidays, I broke the rules of the school and was dishonest in my method of doing so. Asking for permission to spend the holidays with my relatives out of state, I planned that once there, I would go on to spend the bulk of my vacation with my girlfriend who also lived there. My little plan worked. It was a great vacation. Tommy brought his girlfriend home, and I came home with his sister. Their parents made us all feel very welcome. And I'll never forget sitting up late one evening with Tina and finally getting up enough courage to kiss a girl for the very first time. We ended up doing a lot of kissing that weekend, and I thought for sure that I was on the road to success as a man. That was our one and only opportunity to ever physically pursue our courtship.

The next summer something totally unexpected happened. A new girl showed up on campus, and she was in my class, a junior. Never had any girl had such an effect upon me. It was love at first sight. She had dark curly hair, green eyes, and the most beautiful smile I had ever seen. She played the piano like a virtuoso, making me look like the amateur I really was. What a catch she would be! We were meant for each other!

I suddenly forgot about Tina. Bless her heart; she was certainly one of the nicest girls on campus; with wit and humor and personality unequaled. But Lisa! I couldn't explain it. She just seemed to be sent from heaven. It wasn't long before we had become identified as a couple, courting through letters and dating with our eyes. I wrote a note to Tina and, in my youthful ineptitude and inexperience, broke her heart. Her friends told me that she just cried night and day. I felt terrible, but couldn't get over my infatuation with Lisa. Just before school started, Tina's parents showed up and took her away. I was told that she was going away to another school.

"Oh, no! What had I done?" I felt rotten to the core. And I really missed Tina. School just wouldn't be the same without her. Even though I was "in love" with Lisa, I really liked Tina and felt like low-life for what I had done.

School started, and before long the routine had covered up the unfortunate mess I had created. Because of our musical compatibility, Lisa and I were thrown together playing piano and organ for church, switching off from one event to another. We played piano duets, and piano/organ arrangements together. On some occasions, we performed as a trio with my sister's friend Rachel playing the violin.

One of the faculty members, recognizing that Lisa and I were perfect for each other, attempted to assist in our courtship by taking us off campus for organ concerts in some of the large churches in the nearby city. Our not-so-secret romance was sheer bliss.

The only occasion in which we were able to actually touch each other was when I ended up in the sanitarium with pneumonia. Lisa worked there as a nurse's aide. I remember the leap of my heart as the door opened one day, and in walked Lisa like an angel in white uniform with her radiant smile. "I need to take your vital signs," she informed me. She then proceeded to stick the thermometer under my tongue. But when she held my wrist to take my pulse, I thought I had truly died and gone to heaven. As quickly as she had entered the room, she left. And I reclined in the sweet repose of young puppy love.

Shortly before graduation, I was notified that I was valedictorian for our senior class and would receive a small scholarship for college. My picture was even submitted for recognition in the local city newspaper. I was riding high with the feelings of promise and success. Soon I would be off to college. The future seemed to be radiant with promise. Lisa and I could actively and openly pursue our courtship. Our future together seemed certain. I knew, everyone knew, that we were the perfect match for life. Everyone, that is, except Lisa herself.

Just before graduation, I received her "Dear John" letter. I was totally devastated. What I had done to Tina two years earlier was now being done to me. How could something so perfect come to such a screeching halt? And just before graduation? I had never really been satisfactorily able to pursue a relationship with her, because we were so restricted at this school. But next year would be college, and we could really get to know each other. We were the perfect couple! How could this possibly come to an end, and now, just before graduation?

My heart was broken. For the first time in my life, I experienced true heart break. In my free time, I roamed the hills of the farmland and just wept until I could weep no more. For days on end I grieved. Nothing I could say in my letters of appeal to her could make her change her mind. My grief turned to depression and despair. How I finished those last few days of school, marched down the isle to receive my diploma, and held my head high with the dignity of a highschool graduate, I do not know. I had died inside. I had truly fallen in love; my love had been spurned; and I did not know how to go on. All the years of struggling with my unnatural fantasies had been eclipsed by my love for Lisa. If any girl could have ever laid to rest my homosexual tendencies, surely it would have been she.

But it was not meant to be. A wall of protection went up inside me, and though I was to date girls in the future, I was unable to ever find an adequate replacement for Lisa. The love I felt for this girl, I would never again feel for anyone for many years to come. I went into a tail spin of years of pain, turmoil, and confusion. The stage was set for my social failure.

Eleven

From Valedictorian to College Drop Out

More than I realized at the time, my parents really sacrificed and struggled to provide for my education. Though mistakes had been made in the past, and misunderstandings had occurred, their love for their children and pride in their accomplishments were very apparent. When I chose my college, they relocated so that I could live at home and be better able to work my way through. I worked full time in the summers and halftime during the school year to help pay for my own education as much as possible while taking a full load of college courses. I also raised and sold Poodle puppies for a little extra income. In fact, my first car was purchased with fifty dollars and one of those Poodle pups. It was an old '55 Pontiac station wagon that had been wrecked. The front fenders and hood had been replaced and painted with a rust color primer, and the front bumper and grill were missing. It was a real prize, but, it ran great and got me to and from work and school.

Entering college, I really had no idea what direction to pursue in study. Though I thoroughly enjoyed music, I didn't know whether I could make a career of it. Nevertheless, I listed music as my major and proceeded taking the general education requirements along with the emphasis on music.

There were many opportunities to openly date girls, now that I was in college. But I was really soured on dating because of my broken heart over Lisa. I went out with girls usually on school occasions only and hardly ever dated the same girl twice, not really interested romantically in any of them.

On one occasion, however, I labored long over approaching this one special young lady for a date. I thought I could really be interested. With a friendly smile she surprised me by accepting. Her parents were well known in the community and were considered to be quite successful in business; I was from a poor family that was struggling to get all the children educated.

I remember the excitement of pulling up to her house in our old '59 Cadillac. She was so pretty that night and her fragrance was the very essence of spring. We had a lovely evening together, for awhile. It began and ended with a nice dinner out. The perfect gentleman, upon leaving the restaurant I assisted her into the car, walked around and climbed in on the driver's side, and turned the key in the ignition. *RRR-RR-R! Click!* The battery was dead. Not mechanically gifted, I was at a loss. And we were stranded!

Eventually, I was able to find someone to jump the car. When I finally got Carlene home, she was so gracious and kind, thanking me for the night out.

"Good night, Jesse," she said and flashed her winning smile.

I was so ill-equipped to handle embarrassment that I never asked her for a second date, though every time I saw her afterwards she would flash me that friendly smile as though nothing had ever happened. It probably was only an amusing adventure to her that never fazed her opinion of me; but to me, the incident only underscored my ineptitude.

My brother Jake was drafted into the service during my freshman year of college. Home on leave before going overseas to Vietnam, he made a gesture that really surprised me. His pride and joy was his new Yamaha 305. With some foreboding premonition, he came to me just before leaving and said, "Sonny Boy, I want you to have my bike."

"You what? Uh! I'll be happy to take care of it while your gone," I responded.

"No, I want you to have it," he said. With a big brotherly grin and a slap on the back, he added "Enjoy!"

"Thanks, Jake," I smiled back at him. "I'll take good care of it! Promise."

It was an emotional parting for Jake and me. We hadn't seen much of each other in the past few years since being separated by boarding schools, and now the military. I was really going to miss him. So many GIs were coming back home from Nam in body bags. Would this be the fate of my big brother? All thought of sibling rivalry was gone, dead, buried. It never came up again. I really loved this big lug and hoped to God he would someday come back home. I determined that I would keep this motorcycle for him and give it back to him upon his return. "God," I thought, "Please bring Jake back home to us. There's so much "brothering" we've missed out on. Please bring him back!"

Near the end of the first semester of my second year of college, I ran into some personal difficulty. Opening my mail one day, I read a notice from the college administration advising me that unless I could come up with one hundred dollars toward my school bill, I would not be able to take final exams. Not wanting to burden my parents with the situation (knowing of their own financial struggle), and being unable to come up with the money on my own, I began to panic. Soon I found myself unable to concentrate on my studies. Always wanting to excel, and seeing my grades suffering only increased my panic.

Succumbing to the stress of the situation, I stopped attending classes. Every morning, though, I would get up at the same time, gulp down a breakfast, don my leather jacket and helmet, and roar out of sight down the road as if I were going to school. Having Jake's motorcycle as my own had necessitated my getting over that phobia of bikes, and I had actually begun to revel in my new image as a leather clad biker and in the accompanying feeling of the wild freedom I experienced. While my parents assumed I was in classes, I was out riding around killing time, taking in movies, whatever I could find to occupy myself until time to go to work.

Not knowing how to cope with what was happening to me, I decided to leave home. One night I packed a few necessities under my bed with the plan to leave home while my parents went to church. The next morning, they tried to get me to go to church with them as usual, but I refused to get out of bed, "Not today, Dad." This resulted in a little battle of the wills, and I dug in. At the age of nineteen now, I had become a little more assertive and won out in this little contest.

As soon as they drove away, I jumped out of bed, loaded my car, left a note, and drove west. Needless to say, my parents ended up heart broken. All their years of sacrifice seemed to have been spurned. When I talked to my mother on the phone a couple days later, my own heart ached as I listened to her tearful pleas to return and go back to school. Knowing that I was now the cause of her grief, that I had failed her and Dad, was almost more than I could bear. As far as I could remember, I had never before in my life been the cause of my mother's tears. But I felt totally helpless to reverse the direction I had taken. I had already missed the final exams, and my shame would not let me return.

My sister Katie was now married, and she and her husband let me stay with them for a couple of weeks, just long enough to get a job and a pay check and find a room in a boarding house. I worked for a few months as a surgical assistant in one of the local hospitals before receiving my own invitation from Uncle Sam to spend a couple years in his service.

This turn of events, of course, caused great consternation for my parents, for it was during the time of the Vietnam conflict, and Jake was still over there under fire. We never knew if and when his letters would stop coming.

While waiting for my induction, I worked for a few weeks as an ambulance attendant. Having much time on my hands, I decided to paint my old '55 Pontiac station wagon. When I went for an estimate I found that the paint job would cost more than I had paid for the car, (more than fifty dollars and a Poodle pup), so I decided I would just get some spray paint and do the job myself. One of the other young female attendants decided to help me. We got carried away, but the finished product was truly a work of art.

The car was first painted a pale aqua blue. I then cut out stencils and we painted dark green grass all around the bottom and the wheel wells and around the top above the windows. Where others "artists" had stenciled flames coming out from under their hoods, I had grass growing out of mine. The top of the car became a lily pond. Centered on the hood was a huge magnolia. Around the body of the car was a flower bed. Without thinking it through first, I had now become a flower child.

Somehow in all our fun, it had totally escaped me that I would have to sit in this car and drive it around town. I was still raising poodles, and I remember driving around with these poodles hanging out the windows, evoking the startled double takes of fellow road warriors in city traffic. They must have thought I was from some circus. All I needed was the clown suit to make the picture complete.

One day I went to see my uncle in town. He made me park the car down the street. "You ain't parkin' that thang in front of my house."

My father was the same way when later I had to bring all my stuff home in order to go into the service. On one occasion his own car was out of commission. Dad had to drive my car to the airport to pick up another uncle of mine. If that wasn't humiliating enough, on the way he had to stop for gas. Parked under the bright lights of the service station, he discovered that the gas cap required a key! And he didn't have it! What to do, what to do? He decided to break the cap off somehow; and when he did, the lock mechanism fell into the gas pipe and lodged there. He couldn't get it out. By now this slightly overweight, middle-aged, balding, dad had drawn attention, as one can imagine!

At least the cap was off! So, with a pretense of nonchalance he started to pump the gas, only to discover that the pipe could accept merely a trickle because of the obstruction of the lock. Much to his consternation, all he could do was stand there under the bright lights next to the "flower bomb," smile, and wave at the gawkers, and laugh at himself. Dad was learning a lesson in humility.

In later years, this incident has been one frequently revisited with much amusement in our family while reminiscing. This I must say about my father, the unmerciful tease with a warped sense of humor. I admired his ability to see the humor in his own misfortunes and laugh along with every one else at

himself. Unfortunately for me, this character trait was not one
that I was able to develop easily within myself.

Twelve

From GI to Missionary

All I had ever heard about "Boot Camp" could never have prepared me for the reality of it. The "equalizer" (the two minute haircut); the government issue (GI) clothing, everything from underwear to outerwear; the condescending attitude of everyone, civilian as well as military; the "no toleration" schedule for every moment of life; all this served its purpose to reduce me to a non-person and transform me into a mere government issue *expendable* item of military property.

By compliance, and working to not draw attention to myself, I survived Boot Camp relatively in tact in San Antonio, Texas in July! Up until then I had always enjoyed summer camp.

Being non-combatant, from basic training I was advanced into the Medic program. Having had experience as a surgical assistant, I was next accepted into the surgical technicians course, along with my best friend Ray, whom I had coerced into applying. When orders were read at the end of the Medic training, virtually every trainee was ordered to Vietnam, except for the two of us, and a handful who had been accepted into paratrooper school.

Ray and I enjoyed the surgical training immensely, both graduating at the top of the class. Assignments for on job training (OJT) were given according to ranking in class. Having first choice, I went to Fort McPherson in Atlanta, Georgia, and was then able to be home most weekends. Upon completing my training, I tried to prepare myself to receive the inevitable orders for Vietnam. After all, where was someone of my

Military Occupational Specialty (MOS) more needed than close to the battle front? When I received my orders, I nervously tore open the package to discover my orders to South Korea!

"South Korea?" I blurted out. "Are we at war there, too?" I didn't understand, but I didn't complain.

My friend Ray wrote and told me that he had been assigned to Hawaii! Man! How could we ever in the future face our Medic buddies that had all been shipped to Nam? And how many, we wondered, would ever return?

Before I left for overseas duty, my brother Jake returned home from Nam. What relief to have him home safely! Several of my family had been stationed in Nam, and all but one had now returned safely.

It was such a special occasion that day I left for Korea. "Jake," I said to my brother in parting, "I want you to have my bike." I had put many miles on it, but it was still in good condition. He smiled at me and gave me a big hug.

With a brotherly grin and a slap on the back, I added, "Enjoy!"

"Thanks, Jesse," he smiled back. "I'll take good care of it! Promise."

It was still winter when I arrived in South Korea. The sights, sounds, and smells of this far away land were so strange to me, but fascinating. My tour of duty there was to be a thrill, a new adventure for sure. Children were all bundled up and skating with their primitive, homemade ice skates on the still frozen rice paddies. It seemed that everywhere there was a ripe, pungent, putrid smell in the air, though. Upon inquiry I was informed that it was the smell of "kim chee," a vegetable delicacy prepared somewhat like sauerkraut. Eventually, I learned to appreciate it myself, and still do to this day.

Military life wasn't nearly so bad now that I was going to be working in my field of training. I had already been promoted to Specialist 4th Class, which I was a little proud of, having been in the service for less than one year. My assignment was in the 7th Medical Battalion Aide Station in Dong Du Chon, north of Seoul by about two hours rough riding. There was no hospital there, and no operating room (OR), so

I ended up having a rather boring tour of duty. The most excitement I ever had was treating burn patients, sewing up slit wrists and busted lips. The doctors told me to not even call them unless it was something I couldn't handle myself. And I don't remember ever having to call them. I became "Doc."

I was housed in a barracks with about forty other GIs, many of whom had wives back home. It saddened me to see them get caught up in the village activities of bar hopping and whoremongering. But many of these young men, married and single, would fall into the trap of some village girl and maintain a relationship for the duration of their tours of duty.

One fellow who bunked next to me talked me into going into the village to check it out. In the nightclub, I just drank soda pop. He introduced me to a girl named "Tammy" who latched onto me, wanting to become my girlfriend. She was very pretty, but I just wasn't interested in her in that way. Besides, I was still quite confused about my sexual orientation. And being a Christian gave me a very convenient excuse for remaining "undefiled." After several visits and always refusing to drink, she finally threw a glass of rice wine over my head, and that ended our little sterile courtship.

The fellow read into my disinterest what he wanted to, and soon began making advances towards me himself. Though by this stage in my life my sexual orientation was becoming more and more clear, nevertheless, I was repulsed by this fellow and his advances. In my heart, I really wanted to be a Christian. And though my fantasy life was very much alive, overt homosexual behavior frightened me. With all his advances being repulsed, he soon became a very ugly enemy, giving me a real difficult time the remainder of my tour of duty.

On weekends we GIs were allowed to leave the base, and I started going down to Seoul where I discovered a religious GI Center. It was really good to be able to meet other service men of faith, which I still attempted to be. Another interesting factor about this GI Center was that on weekends there were in church attendance young student missionaries from American colleges who were spending a year in Korea teaching English and Bible.

Being a musician, I got involved with these students' religious and social programs on the weekend playing the piano for them, becoming good friends with them and with the director of the school. As my tour of duty neared completion, he asked if I would like to remain in Korea as one of the student missionaries. I jumped at the opportunity, and he worked with the military and with the Korean government to allow my discharge to be in Korea, which was unheard of. But somehow he pulled it off, and I was able to remain, with one condition. I had to be teaching at an accredited college. So they found me a job teaching music in one of the local colleges along with teaching English and Bible in the Language School.

This was a new adventure for me, and I thoroughly enjoyed it. The Korean people, away from the military camps, were very friendly and hospitable. Gracious hosts, they were so honored if we would consent to visit in their homes and eat their food. And their food was truly delightful. The cooks would spend an entire day preparing one of these meals. Visiting in these homes was truly a highlight of my tour in their country.

The students wanted to practice conversational English and were constantly asking us teachers to go on outings with them in our free time. In this way we were able to see many of the sights of Seoul and the surrounding country.

Though I thoroughly enjoyed my teaching, I was never free from the nagging pull of my ever strengthening sexual orientation. Many of our students were young college students, and some of them I found to be very attractive and charismatic. Frequently, I was quite uncomfortable being alone with some of them, because my interest in them became confused between spiritual and carnal. In my heart and mind raged a constant battle between the lusts of the flesh and the fruits of the Spirit.

The director of the school approached me after about four months of teaching and asked me if I would go head up a struggling new school in Thailand. I had always wanted to see the world, and this was really an opportunity I could not resist.

Three other teachers had agreed to go with me for another year of service, all three girls.

A few weeks later, we were on the plane to a new land and a new adventure. Arriving in Thailand, I really experienced a culture shock. It was totally different from Korea. The sights, sounds, and smells were not even remotely similar, though there was one smell that was particularly pungent as had been the smell of "kim chee" in Korea. Riding on the train one night through the jungles, I noticed this stench heavy in the night air. It smelled a little sweet, but also like rotten onions. Later when I asked the missionaries about it, they laughed and told me it was Durian, the king of fruit.

"Yuck!" I thought. "If that's the *king,* then what must the rest of the Thai fruit be like?" Being the brave soul I was, however, I endeavored to learn appreciation for this fruit, and on the third attempt I was addicted. Somehow it had taken on a whole new fragrance and flavor. People started telling me I had been there too long when I began referring to its aroma and taste as like that of butterscotch! And the other fruits of Thailand, why, they were simply delectable: mangos, papayas, lichees, mangosteens, jack fruit, pineapple, and *bananas.* I had never seen so many different kinds of bananas in my life.

The Thai people were much more reserved than the Koreans, and even seemed to be suspicious. Christianity was thriving in Korea, but Buddhism had a very powerful control over the population of Thailand. Teaching the Bible to these students was quite difficult. But we encouraged them to think of these classes as conversational practice classes, and they liked that idea.

Some of the customs and traditions were especially surprising and fascinating. The water festival brought in the rainy season. Wherever we went, people doused us with water. Our school turned into a free-for-all water fight that day. Then there was the barefoot fire-walking at some of the temples. And the day of hallowing the dead, in which the families dig up the bones of their deceased loved ones, clean them, wrap them individually, and then rebury them in an earthen vessel.

While in Thailand I began having a tremendously difficult
time dealing with my homosexual tendencies. The country had
two seasons, hot/wet and hot/dry, but always hot and humid.
The common casual dress of the men was a sarong, a little
wraparound cloth tied at the waist and that was it! I enjoyed
this costume and adopted it myself for around my apartment
and at the beach. The Thai people are beautiful, and I began
suffering mental anguish over my attraction to some of these
scantily clad, physically fit young men. Teaching the Bible, I
was weighed down with the guilt of hypocrisy, though I never,
never acted upon my lustful tendencies. Homosexuality is quite
prevalent in Thailand, and I was frequently assaulted mentally
by the openly suggestive behavior of some of these men; walking hand in hand along the beach, or arm in arm down the
streets, so comfortable in their physical contact and affection
with one another.

I prayed much about my feelings, but seemed to get no
reprieve. It seemed that I was having to fight this battle all
alone in my humanity; but somehow I weathered the storm.

At the end of our year, one of the girl teachers and I
decided that we would travel home together, taking a six week
tour of the Orient in the process. We were very good friends.
In fact, I had become brotherly toward all the girls working
with me. But missionaries and students alike had pretty well
decided that Kathy and I were meant for each other. We weren't!
But it was a little fun playing the game of frustrating the
matchmakers.

A crowd of students and missionary friends accompanied
us to the train station for our departure. We boarded the car,
and as the furnace was stoked, the bell clanged, the whistle
blew, and smoke and steam billowed from the old steam en-
gine as it chugged into motion. It seemed as though we were
reliving some scene in an old western movie, as the smoke blew
past our window. By the send-off of our friends, one would
have thought Kathy and I were leaving on our honeymoon!
But she was perfectly safe with me.

Together we made memories for a lifetime as we visited
missionary stations in Malaysia and Singapore, flew with a

jungle pilot in Borneo, visiting the G-string clad natives in their long houses. We flew back to Bangkok, Thailand and on to Manilla, Philippines, then to Hong Kong, Taiwan, and Korea. Our Oriental tour ended with Japan, then on to Hawaii, before landing stateside in Los Angeles.

Kathy then invited me to go with her for a personal guided tour of the west by car before I caught a plane home to my family in the south. She knew how I enjoyed traveling. We took in Palm Springs, the Grand Canyon, Las Vegas, Yosemite, the Redwoods, and I can't even remember what else. Everywhere we went, family and friends alike believed that Kathy and I were surely going to end up as a married couple.

We really did enjoy each other's company, and, after being together for two and a half years, it was a bit difficult for both of us to face going our separate ways. I loved her like a sister, but that was not a good enough foundation upon which to build a forever relationship. Fortunately for her, I was just not available. For whoever was to end up being my wife was destined for major disappointment and tragic heart break. That thing festering inside me would surely some day come to a head.

——SECTION FOUR——

Having It All; and Then the Fall

Thirteen

Return to Excellence and Having It All

Returning home in late autumn, I joined my family for a great reunion. It took weeks to fill them in on every detail of my two and a half years overseas. I had at least a dozen slide carousels which I thought were spellbinding, but they only put the family to sleep. After all, it was my experience, not theirs, and a few pictures at best would have sufficed.

My tour of duty overseas had inspired me, finally, with a definite direction for my education. To my parents' delight, I had decided to study for the ministry (Dad's one time ambition for himself), and then to go into medicine. My new ambition was to return to mission service as a medical missionary. School was already well in progress, so I would have to wait until the second semester to again take up my scholastic pursuit.

Dad had purchased an old '64 Mercury Comet for me to take back to school. And, after the Christmas holidays, I loaded it up and headed for college. All my high school friends and acquaintances had by now graduated, for I had been out of school four years. So be it. I was not in school for social reasons, but now with a definite aim and purpose in life. I hit the books with diligence and excitement.

In getting set up financially with the school, I discovered to my dismay that before I had dropped out four years earlier, a student loan had been acquired for me. It had taken care of my bill, and, had I known, I could have remained in school. This was unbelievable! Now I was starting all over, with an unnecessary two thousand dollar debt and a whole semester of "Incompletes" that had turned to Fs. I went to the Dean of

Students to plead my case. The debt was unchangeable, but he agreed that I could take all those courses over and replace the Fs with new grades.

What else could I do but go forward? With determination and zeal, I aced everyone of those classes. I was returning to excellence, and it felt great.

Being 24-years-old, I began to think life was passing me by, even though I was accomplishing a great deal in school. Most young college men my age were married. I was still struggling mentally over my sexual orientation and began to reason that if I were to get married, surely that would fulfill all my romantic and sexual desires. Undoubtedly all these other urges would be satisfied.

I was the only one of the six children in my family not yet married. Furthermore, I was older than any of them at the time they had gotten married. Surely, I thought, I was more mature and ready for marriage than any of them had been. Yes! Marriage! That's what I needed in my life. What more could a person ask for?

How could an "intelligent" person be so naive and ignorant? I was twenty-four but obviously not sufficiently intelligent about the nature of the beast I was dealing with. And I certainly was not prepared for marriage. I didn't have anyone lined up anyway. None of the girls I tried dating shared my goals and desires for mission life. They wanted their little yellow houses with rose gardens and white picket fences, and I wanted the adventure and fulfillment of the mission field.

Early the following summer, I received a letter from Leanne, a girl I had worked with in Korea as a student missionary. She had come home to finish college while I had gone on to Thailand with Kathy and friends for another year and a half of service. She wanted to travel this summer and thought about coming through the town where I was going to college. Could she and her brother stop by for a visit?

I responded that of course she could come. It would be great to see her again and reminisce about old times in the Far East.

Soon after that I received another letter; this one from the former director of the language school in Korea. It was a very nice, warm, friendly letter; the first I had ever received from him. He talked about all the other student teachers that had now married each other and were doing so well in advancing their careers. Then, toward the end, he sang the praises of Leanne and suggested that she would be a perfect match for someone like me. Knowing that she was coming to visit, he encouraged more from me than just a reunion of two old friends!

Wow! This was a bit heavy! In all the time I had been in Korea, I had never considered Leanne in that way. Some of the other girls I had dated a little, but not Leanne. She was a very nice girl, however. A ready smile, always cheerful and quick to laugh. She loved to sing and was always willing to participate in church and social activities. Why hadn't I ever thought of her before? Another good quality was that we had the mission work in common, both thoroughly enjoying it.

I began to look forward to Leanne's visit. When she arrived, I saw her in an entirely new light than I had ever seen her before in Korea. She seemed to see me the same way; it was obvious. After visiting with me and my family for about a week, we sat in the car one night before going into the house.

"Leanne," I struggled. "I got a letter from Jerry before you came, and, uh, he made quite a suggestion to me."

"Oh, really?" she acted surprised. "He wrote me, too, a couple months ago and encouraged me to come out here to see you!"

"Well, it sounds to me like he's working overtime doing some match making."

"Yeah," she laughed. "I think we've been set up."

"Well, what do you think? Do you think it would be a good idea?"

"You mean for us to be married?" she smiled with interest.

"Yeah!" I answered cautiously.

"Are you asking me?" [Aw, Man! They just have to do that, don't they?]

"Would you say, 'Yes', if I did?" I could play this game.

"You'll just have to ask and find out, I suppose." She seemed to really enjoy playing this game.

"Okay, will you? Will you marry me?" Did I really say that?

"Yes, Jesse, I think I will."

We were engaged! Just like that! We then decided that maybe she should stay another week for us to get better acquainted and to make wedding plans. School would be starting in four weeks. She was a teacher back on the west coast and would have to immediately resign in time for the school to find a replacement. I was starting back in school at the same time, so we decided that we would get married in four weeks. And we did!

Everything went well for a few months. Leanne was such a good wife and homemaker. We lived in a very small apartment, but she found a place for everything and kept our little home very cozy and neat. I worked halftime and went to school full-time, and Leanne found a teaching position in the area.

But all was not well with me. After the "honeymoon" was over, I began to have less and less interest in physical contact with her. Bless her heart, she had no idea what was wrong. But I got to where I was physically repulsed by her touch and her attentions. I remember thinking that if we had a baby, she would be so preoccupied that she would not need my attentions so much. And I proceeded to talk her into accepting that proposal on the basis that my sister Katie was newly pregnant, and wouldn't it be great if we could have babies close together, so they could grow up to be buddies as cousins.

Leanne fell for it, but with some apprehension. Three weeks before our first anniversary, our little Stephanie was born. What a beautiful child she was! Having a child together really helped me feel closer to Leanne for quite awhile. Now, I really had it all! A godly wife, a beautiful family, and a promising future as I continued to excel in scholastics, maintaining an *A* average.

Upon entering the upper class level, I was assigned to a local church pastor for my on job training (OJT). Applied Theology entailed working with a church. This was quite difficult for me. Not only was I still uneasy about standing before audiences because of timidity, but I also felt so hypocritical in the pulpit, knowing the struggle that continued within me. Invariably there would be someone in the congregation whose presence aroused improper longings within me. Nevertheless, I was well received by the church and successfully completed my assignment.

College graduation was fast approaching, and I was listed to graduate with honors. I had looked forward to this day for a long time.

One afternoon, the head of the Religion Department called me into his office. I was surprised to see two other prominent and distinguished looking gentlemen waiting inside.

"Jesse, I would like you to meet Brothers Jones and Smith. They are here to interview you for a position as Associate Pastor at the Central Church downtown."

"You mean that big one?" I gulped, but did not speak. I couldn't imagine standing up in front of a large congregation with my experiences of stage fright and my feelings of hypocrisy.

I sat through the interview listening to their accolades of my scholastic achievements and their high expectations for someone of my caliber. Then it dawned upon me that graduating with honors resulted in privileges, opportunities, and responsibilities that could be rather intimidating. I was overwhelmed.

Thanking them for their interest, I then announced, to the surprise of the department head, that I planned to complete my pre-med requirements and go on to medical school. Without thinking it through, or, worse yet, without giving it any consideration through prayer and meditation to allow God to show me His will, I turned down the call into the ministry. This may have been a fatal mistake on my part spiritually. For, from that point I experienced a spiritual decline that ultimately terminated in complete and total failure.

My marriage was already in trouble. Outside the marriage bed, I had become more and more passive in my relationship with my wife, finding it increasingly difficult to be loving and affectionate toward her, because it wasn't genuine. My life was a lie, and I knew it. She, in turn, became ever more frustrated and would have weeping spells, asking me if I truly loved her or not. To avoid hurting her, I was constantly lying to her. And I was supposed to be a minister of the gospel!

My guilt was overpowering. I prayed daily, "Lord, please help me to love my wife. This is not fair to her. I don't know how to deal with what's happening to me."

Before long, I was praying, "Lord, please help me to *want* to love my wife."

I was wishing I had never married and began agonizing over the possibility of hurting Leanne and little Stephanie. How could I have ever gotten to this point, teetering on the edge of this precipice. "Lord," I prayed, "Please help me. Please don't let me destroy my home and family and hurt all those I love. Please help me to want to love my wife. Please, create in me a clean heart, and renew a right spirit within me."

After months of such pleading with God and finding no relief from my soul agony, I eventually gave up praying about it any more. What was the use? God did not seem to hear me. I reasoned that I must be too wicked, beyond hope. Perhaps I had grieved away the Holy Spirit.

Bitterness crept into my heart, toward God, for not taking away my overwhelming temptation. Whatever happened to me, it would surely be His fault.

The stage was set. I was a homosexual "in the closet," just waiting for the door of opportunity to open!

Fourteen

My Fall from Grace

On short notice, my wife had to fly out west to be with her ailing mother, and our little Stephanie went with her. I was home alone for the very first time since we had been married. A sense of freedom flooded over me that was exciting yet scary. I wasn't planning on doing anything, but I now realized that I had felt tied down, chained somehow. I experienced a sense of guilt for enjoying my time alone, but soon dismissed it.

Having just completed my pre-med requirements, I was now scheduled to interview for Medical School. One evening while at the college library, I stopped on my way out to browse through a news journal. I picked up a *Time* magazine and was startled to see the cover story. It was about "gay" life in the United States, and the "gay" scene depicted on the cover captured my attention. I found it appealing, rather than offensive, and that unnerved me.

Carefully holding the magazine so that no one could see what I was reading, I turned to the article inside and read with great interest the news of the ever growing and ever more open "gay" movement. Though I had known that, of course, there were people in the world sharing the same homosexual tendencies that I had, yet I had never really met anyone of that persuasion except that weirdo in the army barracks back in Korea. Therefore, I had always felt quite alone with my dark secret, feeling as though no one could ever understand me.

This news article and the pictures of homosexual men in various "gay" hangouts and activities really captivated my attention. I was surprised at the responsive chord it struck within me. And the article actually named some of the more famous "gay" bars in cities around the country. One of them was a place called "Mothers" on Peachtree Avenue in Atlanta.

"Could it really be? I mean, could it really be that close, and that easy, to see what a gay bar was all about?" I wondered. "Oh! But I could never go into a place like that! Or could I? Maybe, if no one knew, and if I could be sure no one would ever find out, maybe someday I could just sneak into a place like that and check it out."

As it turned out, that very weekend I was putting on a musical program at a church near Atlanta. My friend Rachel from high school and her husband had agreed to participate with me, and we had all planned to go down together. However, with a crazy idea in the back of my mind, I notified my friends that I would be driving down alone, "because I had some other business in the area and would not be coming home until the next evening."

We put on a great evening program of spiritual music, and the church was so gracious and appreciative. Afterward, we loaded up all the instruments in my friends' van, said our farewells, and went our separate ways.

My adrenaline kicked in, and I was off for a new adventure. In Atlanta, I was surprised to see Peachtree Streets and Avenues everywhere. Too afraid of what anyone might think, I refused to stop and ask for directions. Instead, I just drove all the Peachtrees until I came upon "Mother's."

Finding a place to park, I sat contemplating my next move for what seemed like forever. Watching the men coming and going, I was struck with terror, having, I suppose, a panic attack. "What are you *doing* here?" I asked myself. "You are a Christian, a married man, a father, trained to be a minister! What are you doing *here*?"

"I'm only checking it out," I rationalized. "I just want to see for myself what it's like to have a crowd of homosexuals all together in one place."

Pulling myself together, I nervously climbed out of the car. Quickly I walked toward the entrance, hoping that no one I knew would see me. "Oh, well," I thought, "what would *they* be doing here anyway?"

The doorman wanted to see my I.D., to my embarrassment. Then he asked for $5.00 cover charge for admission. Hurriedly, I paid him and passed into the darkness of the "gay" night scene. The very building seemed to throb to the deafening beat of K.C. and the Sunshine Band singing, "Shake Your Bootie . . ." The disco lights were whirling and flashing to the beat of the music. The air was thick with the blue smoke of cigarettes. But what left me standing, no doubt with mouth agape, was the undulating scene on the dance floor. I was overwhelmed with the sight of hundreds of men packed together writhing and twisting and "shaking their booties" to the disco beat.

Having never smoked, nor had a drink of alcohol, nor danced, I didn't know what to do with myself. Finally, I went up to the bar and asked for a glass of water.

"No charge, Sweetie," said the bartender smiling sweetly as he swished over to the next customer.

"Sweetie?" I mused. "Sweetie? Is this guy for real? He couldn't be!" But he was. Had I not heard his voice, I would have been certain he was a girl. I had seen effeminate mannerisms before, but never such as this. With amazement, I walked around to a dark wall and watched, and watched, mesmerized by the unbelievable scene all around me.

I nursed that glass of water as long as I could, even dissolved all the ice cubes in my mouth. Not knowing what to do with myself, I went back for another glass of water.

"You're new here, aren't you? My name is Tawilla, and you let me know if there's anything I can do to set you at ease," lisped the bartender.

"Tawilla!?" I laughed inside. But Tawilla, discerning that I felt very much out of place, was making a real effort to help me relax and have a good time. I ended up watching his capers behind the bar as much as everything else going on around me. It was all so new to me, and yet I felt myself being drawn in. For some reason, I couldn't pull myself away from that nightclub scene. When the bar closed at 2:00 A.M., I was still there, had drunk about a gallon of water, and had made countless trips to the toilet.

Tawilla stopped me at the bar as I was about to leave. "Sweetie, I'm having an after hours party at my house as soon as I can get the bar cleaned up. A bunch of "girls" are coming over. Why don't you join us?"

"Girls?" I asked. "I haven't seen any girls here tonight."

"You really are fresh, aren't you, girl?" he laughed with amusement.

I didn't like being called "girl," but somehow coming from this "flaming queen," as someone had referred to him, I took everything into consideration and decided to humor him.

"Well," I said, "I'm not sure."

"Ah, come on. Just stay for a little while, and then go if you like. You're new in town, and I just thought you might like to meet some of the girls."

I consented, to my own shock, but I was really on an adventure here and was very curious as to what these "girls" were all about. When we arrived at his home, there was a group of about ten fellows there, some drinking, some having coffee, some busy in conversation. They weren't girls at all, nor girl-*ly*, but men; nice looking, every day kind of men I would never have suspected of being gay. Tawilla tried to make me feel comfortable there with his friends, but I was really having difficulty, and after a while excused myself to head back home.

Tawilla followed me out to the car, the perfect host, or hostess, I wasn't sure. He wanted to talk a little before I left. "This is your first night out, isn't it?" he asked intuitively.

"Yes, it is." I responded.

"What do you think about it?" he continued.

"I've never seen anything like this in my life."

"Are you gay?" he pried.

"No, I'm not. I just wanted to see what the gay night scene was like."

He continued to probe with what appeared to be genuine interest. He was kind, and he was intelligent. Away from the crowd, he wasn't nearly as effeminate as he had been earlier. I perceived that a lot of that was an act. He was an entertainer behind the bar. The patrons loved it, and he poured it on as well as in.

"I believe you are in the process of coming out," he finally diagnosed. "You really are gay inside, but don't know how to deal with it, right? You've been fighting those tendencies all your life, and they have finally brought you here. Am I correct? Don't be ashamed. Up until tonight, you probably thought you were the only fag in the world, no? Tonight you saw all those hundreds of men in just one gay bar in Atlanta, and you are blown away. And Atlanta is full of gay bars. Sweetie, it's okay to be gay. Accept it! There's nothing you can do about it, so live it and be happy!"

"You're, you're right," I stammered. "Tonight it really hit me. This scene is so far removed from anything and everything I have ever known. But somehow I know that this is probably where I'm going to end up."

It was four o'clock in the morning as I started for home with the sobering realization that I was headed in the very direction of what I had just seen the night before. I was stunned, yet captivated.

A couple days later, I found myself headed into town, on my way to a nursery where a week earlier I had purchased some house plants with my wife. Two fellows operated the business, and one of them I had seen at "Mother's" in Atlanta, so I knew their story. I felt so pulled and drawn by my homosexual tendencies that I began to act irrationally. It is not easy nor necessary for me to detail what happened next. Suffice it to say that I ended up spending the night with one of the proprietors of the business and was initiated into overt homosexual behavior. Afterward, I felt terribly guilty, but hooked. What had been festering in me for twenty years had now erupted with a vengeance. I was totally out of control, and I knew it.

When I called Leslie back the next day, he told me about a local gay bar and disco which I then sought out and began patronizing nightly. Once I fell, I continued to get more and more entangled with the gay night life. It was addictive. I was soon introduced to mixed drinks, and, to my surprise, I enjoyed them. Line dancing was a big thing then, and someone invited me to join the group on the dance floor. "Just follow me," he said, and I did. Being a musician, I caught onto dance quickly and enjoyed the attention it brought me.

In retrospect, I am amazed at how deeply involved I became with this new lifestyle in the four weeks my wife was away from home. I dreaded her return, because I knew that I was going to have to tell her. I knew that our marriage was going to come to an abrupt end, and that it was entirely my own fault. How could I face her? She was pregnant again. What would this news do to her and how would it affect our unborn child? How could I face my precious little girl? I was plagued with guilt, and rightfully so. I felt like the scum of the earth, but totally helpless to reverse the direction I was now headed.

The nearer the approaching return date of my wife, the stranger my behavior became. Filled with remorse, dread, fear, and guilt, I sank into depression. My only reprieve seemed to be the nightclub. It became very difficult for me to sleep, or eat. I seemed to be disoriented with anxiety attacks. My sister Carol Lynn and her husband were living next door to us at the time, and they invited me over for dinner one evening. I tried to be sociable, but my food stuck in my throat. Swallowing green peas became as difficult as swallowing whole eggs. It was obvious to my sister that something was terribly wrong, but I just couldn't talk about it and excused myself from the table.

One night very late I brought a guest home for a "sleep over." He left early in the morning, but not early enough to escape the notice of my sister. She came over to talk to me later and asked what was going on. I could not confess. It was impossible for me to talk about my fall from grace. She, however, let me know with much love and concern, that she had a pretty good idea what was happening. Bless her heart, she wanted so badly to help me, but I could not be reasoned with, and, as kindly as I knew how, I ended the discussion.

In telephone conversations with my wife, it was evident to her that something was terribly wrong. I could not hide my depression and despair, but I dared not tell her over the phone what was going on.

About a week before her return I met Sonny at the club. He was a couple years older than me and living temporarily in Atlanta. We became instant friends and I discovered for the first time the emotional feelings that I should have had all along towards my wife. But they were brought out in me by Sonny, a man. Where I should have enjoyed holding hands with my wife and being arm in arm, I discovered satisfaction in physical affection from Sonny instead.

My whole life was being turned upside down. In this environment I felt normal, and comfortable, and belonging. The turmoil of my life was dissipating, only to be replaced by the remorse and guilt over what I was doing to my family.

When I met Leanne at the airport, her intuition assured her that there was trouble in paradise. Her husband was a different man, a stranger. I endeavored to be the same person, but I was not. I could no longer live a lie. The festering inside me had come to a head, and now had ruptured. There was no turning back.

For a couple of days I refrained from revealing the truth of the matter. But I couldn't put it off forever. Finally, under questioning as to the cause of my deep depression, I broke down and told her everything. We wept together. Her heart was broken, and mine was broken for being the cause of her pain.

Leanne was a trooper, though. She truly loved me and wasn't willing to just give up. Now that she knew the source of our marital problems, she believed we could be mended through counseling. We counseled separately, and we counseled together, for months. Ministers came to visit me, and I went to see ministers. But no one seemed to be able to help me. In the end, Leanne was advised by professional psychologists and psychiatrists, that she would have to learn to live with my orientation; that I could not be changed.

Two very prominent ministers known for their preaching of victory in Jesus, advised her to divorce me. There was no hope for someone like me to be changed. Neither of them had ever met me, nor counseled with me. But they advised her to move on with her life.

Hearing of our family tragedy, my parents showed up to reason with me. I had become the pride of Dad's life, fulfilling all his dreams for himself up to this point. Now he wept on his knees before me. "Jesse, I don't understand. What have I done to make you turn out this way? There's never been anything like this in our family. Where did I go wrong?" he asked in anguish.

At this stage in my life, I hadn't a clue. I had no answers for myself, let alone for my father. I just knew that I was what I was, that I had struggled against it all my life until I could resist it no more. It was too late. God Himself had not been able to help me. What could my parents or anybody else possibly do? I felt immense pity for my parents. Again, I had become the cause of their tears and grief.

Leanne filed divorce papers. I was so ashamed that I couldn't even face the court. So, I basically walked away from everything. The day our divorce was final, our little Donnie boy was born. Ten days later, Leanne moved back to the west coast. As I held that precious little bundle in my arms for that last time and kissed my little Stephanie good-bye, my heart was ripped in two. I felt so sorry for Leanne and the children. For myself, I felt so helpless, so cursed, so abandoned by God. How could He allow all this pain and suffering? Knowing that I was the cause of my wife's pain and that of my children to follow as they realized the loss of their Daddy, I suffered unexplainable anguish myself. But what was I to do? I could no more change myself than a leopard could change his spots, or an Ethiopian could change his skin.

Shortly after my family moved to the west coast, I moved to the east coast with Sonny. In shame and remorse, grief, bitterness, and resentment, I turned my back on everything: my family, my friends, my ambitions, my belief system, and, worst of all, my God. The Jesse everyone had known was dead, as Jesse now began a new life of open sin, blaming God for it all for years to come.

Fifteen

My Gay Life— Censored and Condensed

My father suffered untold grief over the failure of his son's marriage, ambition, and spiritual relationship with God. Everything he had wanted to accomplish in his own life had seemed to be working out in his son's. Once the source of his embarrassment and the object of his teasing and derision, I had, in growing up, become the very apple of his eye. Dad dearly loved and was proud of all his children impartially. But I was the one who had gone into the ministry, a calling he had always wanted to pursue himself. His disappointment and grief was deep and bitter.

After I had moved to the east coast with Sonny, my father was disabled by a massive heart attack. He was only 55-years-old, but his working days were over. The news of this tragedy brought down upon me renewed feelings of guilt and shame. Surely, my breaking his heart had played a major role in breaking his health. Though he has always insisted that it was his own diet and intemperance that brought upon him this affliction, I have never been convinced. The timing was more than coincidental.

Life with Sonny seemed to fulfill an emotional need within me that had never before been met. Being so far away from all my family, friends, and the world I had known made it easier for me to live a life of denial and superficial happiness. We established a home as any other "married" couple, except, of course, there were no plans for children. Sonny and I both ended up teaching school for awhile, which led him back to the university to further his own education.

We went about work and life under the pretense of being just as normal as everyone else, never revealing in the work place that we were gay. In this sense, we were "in the closet," except where his family was concerned. They welcomed me with open arms into their family circle, loved me, and respected me for some unknown reason. It probably was because of my religious culture, to which I no longer adhered, but which obviously had worked to some great extent in making me what I was. Not the homosexual part of me, but the man of clean speech, healthful diet and appetite, with manners and proper etiquette, being kind, considerate and respectful toward others. After all, I still was that same person that needed acceptance, appreciation, and excellence in achievement.

The next summer I came down with pneumonia, though at the time I didn't recognize it. I became so ill that I could not eat and would not drink, nor would I take medication. Sinking into depression, I became totally irrational in that I would not cooperate with anyone's efforts to help me. Sonny became very concerned and tried to get me to the doctor, but I refused. I was so weak and hurting so bad that all I wanted was to be left alone. All he and his family could do was to try to make me comfortable and check in on me once in awhile.

It is a wonder that I did not die. But somehow I pulled through. However, for weeks I was so weak that I couldn't go back to work and could hardly function, except to take care of my personal hygiene and personal needs. In this depression, as I was able to get up and about, sometimes I would get into my car and drive with no destination nor purpose in mind. Floundering hopelessly, I remember pulling into the parking lot of a church one evening, feeling drawn there by some mysterious *Influence*. But no one was there. The church was closed. I suddenly realized how much I wanted it to be open so I could go in and perhaps find some soothing balm for my weary soul. In disappointment, I slowly turned out of the parking lot and headed back home to resume my life as a misfit in society.

The next school year, I learned that Leanne had found a teaching position in the northwest country. As Christmas approached, I felt the tug on a daddy's heart strings and decided to drive out to see my children. Leanne consented to my coming, and Sonny reluctantly acquiesced to my going. Loading up my little VW super beetle with gaily wrapped presents, I headed north and west.

This was my first separation from Sonny, and I felt a sense of freedom and abandon that I rather relished. Stopping for the night in St. Louis, I looked up a gay bar. No one need ever know, I reasoned. I wasn't really looking for anything but a little social time. However, it was a bit of an adventure to be a new face in a new crowd, and to think that I could get away with anything without ever being found out. When approached by an engaging interested party, I enjoyed his nightclub company and later ended up at his house for a "sleep over," falling out of loyalty to Sonny for the first time. Having once yielded to such temptation while I was married, it was not so difficult for me to have the same moral fall again.

A couple of days later I arrived at Leanne's in the middle of the night, and she opened the door of her home so that I might spend a few days with the children. I just had to see the children, even if they were asleep. Tiptoeing into their bedroom, I first stood next to little Stephanie's bed. How beautiful and cherubic she looked in her slumber. Turning over in her sleep, for some reason she opened her eyes and saw me standing there. Her two little arms reached up to me. "Daddy!" she called in quiet surprise.

Bending over to hug her, I melted as those little arms locked around my neck and squeezed me close. How could I go on living without this little angel in my everyday life?

I tucked her back in and watched her go back to sleep before next going over to little Donnie's bed. How big he was now! When last I had seen him, he was ten days old, and that was a year and half ago. He was a total little stranger to me, for I had not been in his life at all and had never bonded with him. But he surely was a handsome child, and I hoped he would take to me in the next few days.

The short time I was in Leanne's home was very therapeutic for me. She wanted our children to know their father, and I was very thankful for her blessed attitude. While Stephanie took to me readily, little Donnie was a bit indifferent. We all played together and had fun, but Donnie had no memory of me, whereas Stephanie did.

Christmas day was a lot of fun. We were all together, like a family, for this fleeting space in time. Leanne was concerned about my well-being and let me know that she was always open for reconciliation if I wanted to come back home. But I couldn't. I was as bound to my new lifestyle as any prisoner who is shackled in chains. Of course, at the time I didn't look at it this way, but it was nonetheless true.

It was with great sadness that I bade farewell to my children and their mother. Again, the feelings of anguish swept over me that I had experienced upon our separation so many months before: I felt so helpless; so cursed; so abandoned by God. How could He allow all this pain and suffering?

On the return home, I stopped again in St. Louis for another sleep over with my new friend. Being unfaithful was really not so hard after all. Arriving home, I resumed my life as best I could as if nothing were amiss. Time and distance helped bury the pain of separation from my children.

Reading the paper one day, I noticed an add that interested me: "Now Hiring, Dance Instructors, Evenings, Will Train." My love for music and my desire to find more work inspired me to follow up on it. The dance studio offered to teach a free class in ballroom dance for potential instructors. At the end of the Bronze class, they would hire those with promise and continue their instruction. They could then teach the Bronze level while taking the Silver. Upon completion of Silver, they could teach Bronze and Silver while continuing on in the Gold, and so forth.

Like a duck on a June Bug, I jumped at the opportunity, having always been intrigued by the grace and beauty of ballroom dancing I had seen on TV and in movies. The training was excellent. We had to be able to lead as well as to follow in order to be all things to all future students. The owner of the studio was the instructor, and I marveled at his style and poise with the Waltz and the Fox Trot. Fox Trot? Now I understood those old records in the attic of our childhood home in the country paradise. Fox Trot was a dance step that worked for innumerable tunes of that particular rhythm.

We also learned the Cha-cha, the Mambo, and the Samba. Mastering the specialized hip motion to these Latin rhythms was great fun. And, of course, there was the Swing. But the craze of the decade was Disco. I could literally dance all night; it was such great fun. With the steps to all these basic dances down pat, I could dance to just about any song there was, for they all fell into one of these basic rhythms.

At the end of the course, I was the one student hired by the studio. Once again I felt the thrill of excellence in achievement. Going on to take my students into exhibition dancing and competitions also served to build up my ego. On these occasions, we usually had the stage to ourselves, and all eyes were on us as we graced the dance floor with our original routines, dressed in tuxedo and ballroom dress. My students' taking home trophies also contributed to my own self-exaltation. But an even greater contribution to self-glory was taking my newfound skill into the gay dancing establishments. I never lacked opportunities to meet people when I was recognized as a good leader in disco dancing.

Sonny decided to go see his parents during school break one semester. I needed to stay home and work. While he was gone, I again practiced infidelity to him after a day at the gay beach with a friend. Having once been unfaithful, it had become easier as yet another opportunity presented itself. It was not something to be proud of, but I did find a bit of excitement in operating on the sly this way. Being sought after, being pursued, was very flattering to my ego. To my shame, I rather enjoyed it.

As the holiday season approached again, I once more experienced the deep longing to be with my children. Leanne had now moved to southern California and again consented to my coming out to visit. Sonny wanted us to spend Christmas together in our own home in Ft. Lauderdale, but he understood my need to be with the children and gave me a good send-off.

Stephanie was now four and Donnie two, and we had a good time together. One day the four of us went to Disneyland. Donnie tired easily, and I ended up carrying him most of the time. By the end of that day, I had become his buddy. He was now old enough to understand that I was his daddy, and, to my great joy, he accepted me. I knew in my heart that I could not go on living on the opposite side of the country from my children. I wanted to be with them, and I wanted to somehow resume my role as not only father to my children, but also husband to my wife. Before leaving, I shared my conviction and desire with Leanne, and she was willing to give me another chance.

With this new resolve, I returned home to Sonny. For the next six weeks, I worked very carefully to ever so gently reveal my plan to him. First, just expressing how much I missed my children; then, conveying how much I wanted to be close to them; and finally, disclosing my desire to move to the west coast. Needless to say, Sonny was at first speechless. In spite of my two episodes of infidelity, which I had later confessed, we were humming along rather nicely in our relationship. We had become more than just lovers; we were real pals. He endeavored to talk me out of going, but he wasn't angry or ugly about it. In the end, we parted as friends with his blessing upon my new venture, and we maintained our friendship.

Two weeks after returning to my children, I knew I could not remarry my wife. I loved her dearly as a person, but I could not fall *in* love with her. My heart could just not change in that way. I was still homosexual to the bone, and I did not want to risk devastating her again. Once was enough. We had both somehow survived our breakup and divorce; yes, terribly scarred, but able to go on as friends.

I had been working on the east coast with a national corporation that had branches in the west. Before taking a leave of absence I had submitted a transfer request with them, and the transfer came through allowing me to set up residence relatively close to Leanne and the children. For the next few years I was able to see the children often and work on building a good relationship with them, until she moved out of state again, to the north.

The flip side of the story is that I also became very active in the gay lifestyle of southern California, flitting, as it were, from flower to flower, seeking out my own self-gratification. Though I had many little romances, I fell into the very common behavior of "tricking," or having the one night stands. At times I felt rather trashy, though I was quite selective in my tricking, of course.

One night I noticed a young man a little older than I enter the nightclub I was patronizing. He seemed conspicuously out of place, as did I according to many who made observation. I introduced myself to him and we struck up a conversation. As it turned out, he was a minister of my same denomination and working at a local Christian college. Even though we both were in and out of gay bars, our religious background and culture made us stand out in the crowd somewhat to discerning people as not really belonging in a place like this.

Don was his name, and we became good friends over a period of time, which developed into somewhat of a romance. He introduced me to a religious gay organization he was involved in, and we attended some of their functions. But I never could join it. To me, homosexuality and religion could no more mix than oil and water. I knew what the Bible said about us. I had left religion behind, refusing a call into the ministry, because of my feelings of hypocrisy. In my understanding, attempting to maintain a spiritual life while hanging on to the gay life was nothing more than an exercise in futility.

Besides, I could see in Don a perpetual conflict, the law in his mind warring against the law in his members, to quote from Romans 7. He was trying to hang on to the best of both worlds, the kingdom of this world and the kingdom of heaven, at the same time. But the Bible says we cannot serve two masters, for we will hate one and love the other. I didn't need this additional conflict in my life. Being steeped in my life of sin, and carrying its weight of guilt, I had not the added burden of the guilt of hypocrisy. I had relative peace compared to

Don who seemed to be in that uncomfortable position of strad-
dling the fence.

I continued my life of little romances here and there with
no strings attached. This allowed me the freedom to come and
go as I pleased with whomever I pleased without getting any
flack from anyone.

But then I met Angelo, and my shopping days were over.
It was with him that I entered into my second long-term
monogamous relationship. With him, I attempted to settle
down once again and bring some stability and sanity back into
my life. His family, like Sonny's before, opened their hearts
and homes to me, accepting me as one of the family. We spent
all the holidays together, partied together, and did all the things
that any other family would do. They flew me to Hawaii as the
family photographer for Angelo's brother's wedding. On another occasion, we all flew together with his charming little
grandmother to Vera Cruz, Mexico to the home country of her
childhood. (Angelo told me his father was Italian, but his
mother's mother was from Vera Cruz).

I was so attached to this family that when our relationship
ended up on the rocks five years later, it was the family that I
missed the most. We never stopped loving each other.

It was over Angelo that I had eventually come to pray,
"God, if you will get me out of this relationship, out of this
mess, I *promise* I will go straight and never have another homosexual experience for the rest of my life."

But once free, as with the old covenant promise of the
Israelites, my promise was quickly forgotten, and I continued
on in my mad career of self-exaltation, self-advancement, and
self-gratification.

Sixteen

On the Rebound

San Diego was one of my favorite cities. Beautiful climate, beautiful city, beautiful people. It was here that I was first inspired to take up the sport of hang gliding. As I lay basking in the sun on Black's Beach, one of my favorite hang outs, I was fascinated by the hang gliders that launched from the cliffs and soared directly overhead up and down the coast, their beautiful colors being illuminated by the brilliant sunlight. Having once been a private pilot myself, I longed to be back in the air and eventually pursued that ambition to become a hang glider pilot.

There was another reason I enjoyed San Diego so much, and that was its night life. The gay bars and nightclubs were very popular and well patronized. It was on a Saturday night; I was in my glory dancing at a country/western gay nightclub. Line dancing and clogging were my favorite, though most of the dancing was the two step with a partner, very similar to the ballroom fox trot.

This little pastime of mine really helped feed my ego. Incorporating my ballroom style into my country western dancing gave me an expertise much admired by onlookers. It was so good to be noticed and praised!

One person stood out in the crowd this particular Saturday night. Every time I rounded the corner where this clean cut, very handsome fellow stood, I noticed him watching me intensely with a smile of admiration. After a few more songs and dances, I mustered up enough courage to ask him if he would like to dance.

"Oh! I've never done this before", he replied.

"Come on!" I urged, seeing his interest. "I'll teach you. It's easy!"

With a smile he consented, and off we went. Carefully, I stuck to just the simple basic step, nothing fancy. I could tell that he was really enjoying his dance lesson. We spent the rest of the evening dancing together, and getting better acquainted.

Mark was a fascinating individual. It was obvious that he was well educated and had a lot of class. We became instant friends and agreed to meet each other same time, same place, next weekend. In the ensuing weeks our relationship progressed from dance partners, to good friends, to lovers. He was a musician, and, having that in common, we performed together at various functions. He progressed rapidly with his dancing, and we became very recognizable as dance partners.

Intellectually, Mark was a genius. His IQ had been determined as immeasurable, according to him, and I believed him. He had developed an educational program for gifted children that was highly acclaimed; in fact, he was director of his own school for the gifted in San Diego.

As the months progressed, we became more and more bonded to each other. We also both experienced a drastic increase in our gasoline bills as he came to Los Angeles to spend a weekend with me, and I went to San Diego to spend the next with him. Soon we had exchanged house keys, in order to be able to make ourselves at home at either one's domicile. We mutually shared our desire to enter into a monogamous relationship, and I truly believed that I had discovered "Mr. Right."

One night, in one of our conversations we were sharing our backgrounds. I mentioned that I had been born into and raised within a Christian home and shared with him some of my religious beliefs, admitting that they were not active in my life. He was noticeably disturbed. As we continued to share, he finally said, "Jesse, this will never work."

"Why?" I asked. "What does my past have to do with anything. Obviously I'm not living in harmony with anything I was raised to believe in. So, what difference does all that make?"

"This just isn't going to work out" he responded, shaking his head.

The subject was changed, and before long it seemed as though nothing was wrong. The topic was never brought up in discussion again. We continued our weekend relationship for months, and we seemed to be getting increasingly attached to each other as time marched on.

One San Diego weekend, we were having a little social gathering in his home. The entertainment began to shift into a direction that made me very uncomfortable. Mark began reading tarot cards for the guests. This led to some other games that revealed to me the possibility that he was psychic and involved in the occult. Other mysterious objects and activities of his that I had observed in the past now seemed to appear rather sinister.

But the evening ended on a light note with all of us a little under the influence of one thing or another. Soon, all was dismissed in my mind as irrelevant. Why should any of that interfere with our romance? So, we continued on.

Valentines Day fell on a week day this new year. I had the bright idea of taking a dozen red roses to San Diego as a surprise. Arriving in the evening, I used my key and let myself in. "Lady," the collie, barked in surprise as an unexpected guest was letting himself into her house.

"Shh! Lady, hush! It's just me." I whispered.

Recognizing me, she ran over for some lovin'.

Just then the door to the bedroom opened, and out came Mark to find me standing there with the dozen red roses. Something was wrong! Normally he would be radiant with delight. Instead, he . . . oh, no! Surely not!

"Jesse, I . . ." he struggled for words. "I'm sorry! I wasn't expecting you! Can you please wait here a minute?" And he disappeared back into the bedroom.

It seemed he was in there forever. I knew what to expect, but in stunned disbelief I could not move. I didn't know what to do. My world was falling apart.

When he finally returned, he knelt down on the floor, buried his face in my lap and wept. Eventually he regained his composure. "Jesse, there is somebody else in the bedroom. I am so sorry to have done this to you."

The drive home seemed endless. I hadn't realized that I had finally, after twenty years, let my barriers down to the point where I could be hurt. Up to this point, all the hurt had been caused *by* me. I sank into depression and despair such as I had not experienced since receiving the "Dear John" letter from Lisa, my high school sweetheart. In fact, I recognized my feelings as such. For weeks I grieved over the loss of my loved one. I grieved as over one who had died. In my depression, I was quickly becoming dysfunctional.

One morning the telephone rang. It was on the weekend, so it couldn't be a call for a sales appointment. "Who would be calling this time of morning?" I wondered. Reluctantly I picked up the phone.

"Hello?"

"Hello! Jesse, is that you?"

"Yes! Carol Lynn, is that you?" I hadn't heard from my "little sister" in quite a long time.

I wondered why she wasn't in church, for she was a faithful church member, and by this time of the morning she would normally not be home. As I attempted to carry on a cheerful conversation, she interrupted me.

"Jesse, what's wrong?"

"Why do you ask that?" I responded cheerfully.

"Jesse, something is wrong. I can hear it in your voice."

Carol Lynn and I had always been very close. We could read each other like a book. And there was no way for me to pull one over on her this time. At that, I broke down, no longer able to maintain control of my emotions. I explained the panic I was experiencing in my depression which was leaving me dysfunctional.

"Would it help if I came out to see you?" she asked. "We just sold our old dump truck and I have a little money for airfare."

I tried to make her believe I would be all right. But she refused to take "no" for an answer saying she would call me right back and let me know when to pick her up at the airport.

Two days later, Carol Lynn was in California. What a blessing she was to me! Being a Christian, she, of course, did not approve of my lifestyle. However, like Jesus Christ, her love for me was unconditional. And that is what I really needed in my depression and despair, to not only know that someone loved me unconditionally, but to have it demonstrated. Her coming out was no little sacrifice for a country mother living up in the mountains of Tennessee.

The two weeks she spent with me was just the therapy I needed. I rebounded very quickly with her in my home and sharing my life for that little window of time. I had a desire that Carol Lynn would truly accept me for who and what I was, regardless of her disapproval of my lifestyle.

"Carol Lynn," I asked one evening. "Would you go with me somewhere?"

"Where?" she asked skeptically.

"Would you go out dancing with me tonight? I know, you've never danced before in your life, and you don't approve of the places I go. But, just this once, would you go with me? This would be very special to me."

"Jesse, you know I don't go to places like that!" she reacted. "And, besides, I really would make a fool of myself."

"No you wouldn't!" I pleaded. "I'm a good teacher. You just hang on and enjoy the ride. Pleeeeze?" I begged.

"Well, all right. Just this once. But, boy! What would the people back home at church think if they saw me out dancing in a gay nightclub?"

It was early in the week on a slow night at the club, and on top of that we went real early so that I would have time to teach her a few steps before the place got crowded. I knew she would be uncomfortable if there was an audience.

Carol Lynn and I had a great time that evening two-steppin' around the dance floor to the nasal twang and wailing laments of Patsy, Dollie, Tammy, Winona and Naomi, Loretta, George, Dwight, and Willie, add infinitum. But I never was quite able to get all the "hitch out of her giddy-up." Dancing was so foreign to her.

As the evening progressed, some of my bar friends showed up, and I introduced them to my sister. These California urban cowboys were quite intrigued by this little "belle o' the south". Carol Lynn had never really been around homosexuals. But she was a hit with them, and they revealed themselves to her as real people who had feelings and emotions and every day concerns like other every day people. She could see them as people who outwardly appeared as normal as anyone else; people of wit and humor and education, commoners and professionals. Her reaction to them was one of unconditional love and acceptance. Not approving of the lifestyle, she could still relate to them as real people, lovable and fun to be around; recognizing, of course, that the gay society included a full spectrum of personalities; a cross cut of society in general.

On occasion, Carol Lynn would wait out a few dances, conversing with these new acquaintances while I participated in the line dances and clogging specials, or danced with someone else. Always aware of the bystanders, a new face in the crowd caught my attention that night; not only because he was a new patron, but because he stood out in the crowd with a unique genuine country boy look, and his attention seemed to be locked in on me. But, I was out on the town this night with my sister, so I dismissed the impulse to get acquainted with someone new.

Carol Lynn's two week visit was much too short, but she had a family who needed her back home. By the time she left, my spirits had been much bolstered. It was so good to have family that loved me so much, even though I knew I was a total disappointment to them. When I allowed them, they really reached out to me to demonstrate their unconditional love, also showing a genuine interest in understanding me better; understanding who and what I really was.

Totally over my depression and with broken heart on the mend, I picked up all my little pieces and resumed life. Of course that meant hitting the dance floors on a weekly basis, and sometimes even nightly. Each night of the week was a special night at one gay club or another. While all the other week nights might result in mediocre patronage, Tuesday night at "The Rawhide" in Long Beach was the night to arrive early if you wanted to get in at all.

So Tuesday night early, there I was. And so was Andy. Who was Andy? Andy was that new face in the crowd who had caught my attention the night I was there with my sister a week earlier. As on that night, so again as an onlooker, his attention seemed to be locked in on me while I was dancing. Eventually I approached him and invited him to join us on the dance floor.

Andy was 27-years-old, freckled, with shoulder length sandy blond curly hair, brown eyes, and a grin that just wouldn't quit. A straw cowboy hat cocked back on his forehead revealing gold ringlets, and a turquoise bandana tied around his neck, he really had the look of country. From Kentucky, he spoke with a southern drawl so thick you could cut it with a knife. I could just picture him sittin' on a hay stack, chewin' on a straw, and whittlin' on a stick.

He lit up a cigarette, then took it from between his pearly whites and offered it to me. "What kind of a gesture was that?" I thought. "This must truly be southern country manners. No one had ever extended me this courtesy before." I was charmed by his unique style, and his unaffected country manner. And, though I smoked very little myself, with intrigue I accepted his polite courtesy.

As had Mark from San Diego, Andy told me that he had never done any country/western dancing before, so I offered to teach him. We were inseparable the rest of the night. He seemed to catch on pretty quickly and asked if I would give him lessons. So we started meeting at the club nightly when it first opened and no one was there so that I could give him concentrated lessons without distraction.

As it turned out, he had been an exhibition disco dancer with a girl friend back home in Kentucky, and had even been on television! But he had never done country/western. Being a man, he had been the lead dancer. Now, being in a new field, he had to be the follower. He was a quick learner, and in two weeks we had become a country/western dancing team with that unusual ball room style that evoked the admiration of the nightclub scene wherever we went. We both reveled in this little bit of glory.

We also became very quickly romantically involved. I was on the rebound. In virtually no time, realizing our compatibility and our mutual desire for companionship, we moved him into my home and began our life together as a monogamous "married" gay couple. We were so right for each other that we became the envy of those still looking in all the wrong places for their own "Mr. Right."

The longer we were together, the more we felt that our relationship was truly "'til death do us part." I became well acquainted with, and accepted by, *his* family too.

Andy had moved out to California to reestablish a relationship with his mother who had abandoned him in childhood. He told me about being left alone by his mother at his grandmother's house at the age of two and a half. Somehow, he found his way back to his mother's home in the same little town, only to find the door locked. Hearing the voices of his mother and some man inside, he banged on the door, only to hear his mother urge, "Shh! It's Andy. Be quiet so he'll think no one is here." Though he persisted, no one ever opened the door. When his grandmother later came home, she found her abandoned grandson sitting up on top of her piano in the fetal position in total hysterics. From that point on, he was raised by his grandparents.

Twenty-five years later, when his grandparents had passed away, he decided to move to California and look for his mother. He was not prepared for what he found, but wanted her in his life, nevertheless.

By now she had remarried several times, had several more children, now grown, and was an alcoholic bartender. She was a friendly little lady, and quite pretty, but totally messed up. In her youth she had been a Miss Kentucky. She had married Andy's father, a career man who eventually became vice president of one of the largest national corporations. Her life now, however, was a pitiful scene. She lived in a camper trailer in a little park not far from the bar. Every night after work she would drink herself into a stupor and pass out. Andy felt much compassion for her and wanted to be near her and help take care of her, which was commendable. I admired this in him.

Our relationship over the next three years seemed to be working so well that I didn't notice how I was being pulled down deeper and deeper into vice and intemperance. Andy himself was alcoholic. He started his day with Bloody Marys and ended his day with Bourbon and Coke. The thoughtful, caring, country gentleman, he was always offering me something to drink. When lighting up a cigarette, he would invariably pull it from between his teeth and give it to me, then light up a second one for himself.

Up until this relationship, I had been fairly serious about my health and my physical appearance, even though I did keep some late hours. And though I maintained that fetish for looking good, once I started smoking regularly and drinking more and more, socially of course, then I was no longer able to keep up with my physical workout routine. But that was all right. I was comfortable in a very suitable relationship. I was growing older every year and it was all right to relax a little more and not take everything so seriously.

I really settled into this relationship, forgetting the promises of the past that I would give up this lifestyle and go "straight."

But the Lord was not willing to leave me at peace in this my "perfect" situation. One night I was startled out of my sleep by a terrible nightmare.

"What is it?" Andy queried groggily, being himself shaken out of sleep by my sudden rude awakening.

"Nothing, really," I answered. "I just had a bad dream. Go back to sleep. I'm all right."

Then I pretended to go back to sleep, so he wouldn't press me on the nature of the dream. Actually, I lay there experiencing once again all the horror of being lost at the coming of Jesus in the clouds of glory.

"Why do I keep having this dream?" I thought. "I know I'm lost. But what can be done about it? I am who I am and what I am, and there's nothing that can be done about it!"

Eventually, once again I was able to drift off into that fitful sleep that always succeeded my recurring dream.

SECTION FIVE

The Long Journey Home

Seventeen

I Just Called to Say "I Love You"

Over the years that I lived the "gay" life, my parents periodically found occasion to visit me. To the amazement of my friends and lovers, my Christian parents were willing, if not indeed anxious, to visit with me in my home, and to even stay extended periods of time under the same roof.

My understanding of Dad was quite different in my maturity than the perception I had of him during my childhood. The unconditional love that he and my mother both demonstrated toward me as a homosexual and toward my circle of friends was quite unexpected of Christians, for it was common knowledge that homosexuality was considered to be an abomination in their belief system.

Mom told me how she could see in the eyes of my friends a deep longing for acceptance and approval. And her motherly instincts just reached out to them. She and Dad both were drawn to my friends in love and sympathy. Their interest was genuine and was recognized as such. My parents were, therefore, always accepted, appreciated, admired, and loved in return by my homosexual friends and lovers. I could see that, like Jesus, though they hated the sin, they genuinely loved us the sinners, and this had a profound impact upon me.

It was quite certain to me that I would always be homosexual; that I was born that way and would remain that way forever. Knowing that I could never change myself, nor could I be changed, I wanted an opportunity to really help Dad come to grips with reality on this point. I really needed him to understand me and to accept me for who and what I was and would always be. I desired confirmation of a mutual love and acceptance between us. My mother and I had always had a comfortable relationship, but that between my father and I still seemed at times somewhat uncomfortable, though I knew he really loved me.

On one occasion, when my parents were traveling in California, they were visiting a few days with my sister before coming to stay with me. At the time, I was managing a team of salesmen in the five southern California counties around Los Angeles. As I was driving the freeway to San Diego one evening, I had an urge to call my father to set the stage for working out this mutual understanding and acceptance. Picking up the car phone, I called my sister's phone number and asked if I could speak to Dad.

"Hey! What's up?" Dad greeted.

"Hi, Dad!" I said. "I just wanted to say, 'I love ya!' "

"Ehh?" Pretending to be all of a sudden hard of hearing, Dad could not hide the awkwardness he suddenly felt to express himself.

"I just called to say, 'I love you!' " I repeated clearly, knowing that he had heard explicitly the first time.

"What's that you said?" he now asked playfully. But his emotions were beginning to show through as I detected tears in his voice.

"Dad," I repeated, "I just called to tell you that I love you!"

"I love you, too, Jesse," he broke down crying, no longer able to disguise his emotions behind his incurable mischievous humor.

"Dad, I'm on my way to San Diego, and on the way back through Los Angeles I'd like to stop and see you. There's something I need to talk to you about."

"Yeah, yeah. Okay!"

"Bye, Dad!"

"Bye, Jesse."

Oh! That felt so good. I really loved my father with all my heart. We had been at odds with each other at times in the past, yet it was quite apparent that he really had loved me and had been proud of me all along. In spite of his faults, he had demonstrated that love in so many ways throughout my life. However, rather than holding on to all the good memories that were available for me, I had instead harbored resentments and bitterness over unfortunate incidents of his behavior, quite often triggered by my own peculiar conduct, allowing these incidents to overshadow all the evidences of his genuine sacrificial love for his family, which was an evidence of his real character. He had worked hard and sacrificed much to keep all his children in church school, well clothed, and well fed.

Most of our bad experiences were not due to malicious intent on his part at all, but to a sense of humor that I had neither understood, nor appreciated. His mistakes, I could somewhat understand, had been due to his own abusive upbringing, his lack of education in the skill of child training, oblivion to my emotional confusion, as well as to his lack of self-control.

I wanted my father's forgiveness for the pain and disappointment I had wrought in his life. And I wanted him to know that I truly loved and appreciated him.

Returning home the next evening, I stopped at my sister's residence to visit my parents. Walking into the house I greeted Mom and Jeanie, then asked, "Where's Dad?"

"He's in bed," Mom answered pensively.

"In bed? Why so early?"

"Well, he said he wasn't feeling too well. Actually, I think he's suffering some anxiety about facing you right now."

"Why?" I asked. "All I told him on the phone was that I loved him!"

"Well," Mom hesitated. "He came and asked me what I thought you wanted to talk about; what you wanted to get off your chest. I didn't know what to tell him. He worried about it so much that I finally told him what you shared with me last year about the trauma you felt over that birthday card at your twelfth birthday. He couldn't remember it, but was so filled with remorse that the next thing I knew he had retreated into the bedroom and hasn't come out since."

"Oh, no!" I replied. "I had forgotten all about that! And, really, it had nothing to do with my phone call!"

"Well, you better go in there," she said. "He really needs to talk to you."

I went directly into the bedroom and found Dad propped up in bed reading. When he saw me he just broke down and wept.

"Jesse, can you ever forgive me for all that I did to you when you were growing up?" he cried, unable to contain his grief. He was so truly contrite, all I could do was hug him and cry with him.

"Dad, I forgave you a long time ago. I've known for a long time that you really love me. I didn't want to talk to you about all the details of our past. I just want you to accept me now; to love me and to understand me and accept me for who and what I am now; as I am. I want us to have a mutual love and respect for each other, and to have a good father/son relationship."

On that very day, a weight of unrealized anger and resentment rolled off my back that had been with me all my life. Dad and I were reconciled. Nothing bad that had ever happened in the past had any weight with me anymore. That doesn't mean that I was suddenly struck with amnesia. But I now realized that unconditional love could outweigh any unpleasant and unfortunate circumstance of life. I felt a new freedom that I had not even realized I had been without.

Unaware of it at the time, this occasion was of major significance in my life. The relationship between my father and me was in a rapid healing process, and we would go on to later become the closest of friends. Conditions were ripening for my long journey back home. But being the hard study that I was, there were a few more lessons yet to be learned. I had not yet bottomed out.

Eighteen

As the Twig Is Bent...

There is an old adage that says, "As the twig is bent, so grows the tree." The author of the adage? I'm not sure. Nevertheless, I have come to believe it to be true. My years of living in the world of homosexuality had been spent, up to this point, not only in self-exaltation, self-ambition, and self-gratification; but worse, self-justification and blaming God. But, could it be that as a twig I had been bent? Could I possibly be the product of circumstances and environment? And if so, what difference did it really make? I was still the same homosexual, regardless.

A number of well-intentioned, concerned Christian friends, family, and acquaintances had made attempts to arouse within me an awareness of my danger of being eternally lost, and to point me to the way out of my lifestyle by telling me it was not in harmony with God's original plan for man; that it was not in accordance with *His* will, but a result of *my* own *choice*. Therefore, I could *choose* to be "straight," with God's help of course, if I really wanted to be straight.

"*Choice!*" I would react. "Do you think any one in his right mind would *choose* to be homosexual? to live a life so socially unacceptable? to be the object of ridicule, scorn, and disgust? to be shunned and reviled? If so, why?

"No! I did *not choose* to be this way. I was born to be this way. I've been this way ever since I can remember. I was just always too ashamed to admit it. But it finally became so big within me that I had to come out and accept it. You just don't understand!"

After fifteen years of these attempts to justify myself, however, the reality of the consequences of being homosexual began to settle in upon me. Though I was very settled into my "marriage" with Andy, very few monogamous relationships seemed to be " 'til death do us part." (This being the voice of experience as well as observation). Quite often the long-term "marriages" involved infidelities in order to keep excitement in the sex life, and they ceased being truly monogamous. The most pitiful cases of homosexuality seemed to be those who were aged and no longer with a significant other, no longer physically attractive and desirable. They seemed doomed to lives of loneliness, finding fulfillment as spectators of life rather than actively participating anymore. One's attractiveness and desirability seemed to wane with age. And I, like everyone else, was not getting any younger.

The AIDS epidemic had sprung up. One of the most sobering experiences of my gay life was the Los Angeles Gay Pride Parade with attendance in the thousands. One platoon of participants consisted of AIDS victims attempting to achieve recognition for their cause. In shock and pity, I watched these beautiful people, their comeliness marred by purple skin splotches from face to feet, marching with banners held high. Realizing they all would soon be dead was most unsettling, heart-rending, and touching. In the ensuing years, I personally knew a large number who suffered this tragic fate.

Another platoon of participants were gays and their parents carrying banners and placards such as "My Son Is Gay, And That's Okay!"

"Could they really mean it?" I questioned in my heart.

My own life seemed to be following a downward, spiraling path toward self-destruction. Having been raised a Christian, I had been well taught the many and varied consequences of smoking, drinking, drug abuse, general intemperance, and illicit sexual activity. My own future began to appear rather dismal.

As I considered my recurring dream of the coming of Jesus, it was no new revelation to me that I was in a lost condition. Fifteen years earlier, I had chosen to "come out of the closet," to be openly lost rather than to be lost as a hypocrite. However, the eventual effect of "the dream" was that of shaking me from the state of denial into that of facing reality. The horror I experienced in those dreams of facing the all-searching, all-knowing gaze of Jesus was beyond my ability to put into words. Being forever lost was much worse than I had once imagined.

"But, what was I to do about my lost condition?" I agonized. "I was not responsible for who and what I was. I was born this way. Everything was God's fault," I attempted to console myself.

Soon realizing that casting all that blame upon God was only my feeble attempt to escape accountability for my own actions, I finally began a process of self-analysis, scrutinizing my life from childhood, in an attempt to understand my state of homosexuality; carefully at first, because it was too shameful and painful.

"Could it really be my own fault?" I questioned. "Could it really be that I am homosexual because of *my own choices?*"

"No! It could not possibly be!" I argued with myself. "I did not *choose* to be the way I had turned out to be. I had made all the *right* choices, until finally I could no longer deny who and what I really was inside.

"I always wanted to be good, to be accepted and appreciated, and to excel. Therefore, I *chose* to be, to the best of my ability, the kind of person that would be accepted, appreciated, and admired.

"Why!" I continued to argue. "Had I not *chosen* a Christian education for myself, in high school and in college? Had I not *chosen* to be a missionary in my youth? Had I not *chosen* to study theology, even graduating with honors?

"I had *chosen* to be married to a Christian woman. I had *chosen* to have little Christian children. I had *chosen* to establish a Christian home.

"How could someone like me who had made all these *right* choices along the way, who had *chosen* to follow the blueprint for happiness within the guidelines of God's *chosen* people, end up so far from God so quickly?" I reasoned.

An honest look at myself brought to me the realization that fifteen years earlier I had become overwhelmed with temptation to follow evil tendencies that I had been fighting all my life. Even though I had prayed relentlessly for God to "create in me a clean heart," and to "renew a right spirit within me," and to save me from falling into a life of sin that, to my understanding, allowed no turning back, I never recognized an answer to my pleas for Divine help. In the end, I had just stopped praying and given up, fallen into sin, lost my family, left my church, and, in deep bitterness, blamed God for my fall all these ensuing years. *He* had not come to my rescue. It had never occurred to me before that my fall into this life of sin had only taken place *after* I gave up praying for deliverance. And I had given up because I had not been delivered from *temptation*. Could it be that it was not God's fault after all? Could it be that the fault was truly my own for not continuing to resist in prayer?

*   *   *   *   *

Over a period of time, I continued my soul searching and self-analysis. As I began to painfully peel back the layers of my life in order to closely examine myself, I could not help but wonder if my childhood introduction to sex (and that perverted), could have any bearing upon the direction my life had taken.

I discerned that the day of my introduction to sexual activity at the age of four might be of key significance in understanding my childhood development and growth as a human being. With nothing else to measure against, the memory of the incident with all its vivid details had festered in my mind. The fact that I felt too dirty, too guilty myself to tell my parents or any other living soul about the incident, left me totally alone to sort it all out and to try to make sense of it all. And that is one mental and emotional load that, I dare say, no 4-year-old child is equipped to handle. I was left feeling peculiar and abnormal.

To add to all my distress was the fact that from a very early age I found myself having romantic and even sexual fantasies, abnormal ones, toward men. Very likely, this is not unusual for a boy who has been sexually molested by a man. My introduction to sexual behavior was by a young man, and it was perverted sexual behavior. And, as that was all I had to relate to sexually, I found myself frequently reliving in my mind the incident in the big farm truck under the tree out in the wheat field.

Perverted sexual fantasies plagued my mind from that age of four onward. I felt very guilty but seemed to have no control over my thoughts. It was difficult for me to identify comfortably with manhood. In a way, I feared men, and at the same time was strangely attracted to them with a fascination that somehow did not seem normal. I longed for their approval and for their physical affection, yet felt guilty for my longings. I was terribly confused by my emotions.

As the idea of sexual behavior rolled about in my mind every living day, with no outlet and no expression, no guidance, nor instruction, it continued to fester, seeking some way of surfacing, some way of expression. Along with this mental turmoil, I experienced much guilt even as a little child.

Prior to that first sexual encounter, I have no memory of a bed-wetting problem. In fact, my parents have confirmed that all of their children were potty trained before the age of three, and I was no exception. They were baffled at my sudden regression at the age of four. At the age of nine, they had taken me for a medical examination and the doctor assured them that there was nothing wrong with my kidneys. I was physically sound.

As I continued looking deeper and deeper into my life experience, it began to dawn on me that in keeping that deep, dark secret, in suppressing the trauma of my childhood sexual initiation, I might just have created an emotional disturbance that manifested itself in a physical way through lack of bladder control. Of course, as a child, even as a teenager and young adult, I certainly did not make any connection between the two at all.

Being neither a psychologist nor a psychiatrist, I knew not whether my self-analysis would hold up under scientific scrutiny. However, in looking very closely and even prayerfully at my own life experience, honestly seeking understanding, I began to see and believe there was a connection, whether science would back it up or not.

After all, science does not have *all* the answers! The predominant scientific community is still spending billions of dollars to support their unscientific theory of evolution that was eventually renounced by the very scientist with whom it originated. For to acknowledge Creation would be to acknowledge accountability to the God of Creation. And rebellious hearts will go to any lengths to justify self and avoid moral accountability. (Did I say that?) That's not much unlike what my own rebellious heart had been doing for years!

My emotional disturbance probably worked against me, causing abnormal sensitivity and a warped perception of reality on my part. Rather than being able to go with the flow, spring back with resilience, and laugh along with others at myself, I instead mistook teasing and mischief as ridicule and scorn and harbored resentment and bitterness.

My regression into bed-wetting was tolerated at first, for I was just a little boy. My mother was frustrated with my problem, but never made me feel shamed, never embarrassed me. She worked with me, and, though quite disappointed at times, she never belittled me.

On the other hand, I did feel an ever increasing sense of ridicule and scorn on the part of some of my siblings and my father. It hurt coming from my siblings, but it was devastating coming from my father. It seems as though this derision tended only to exacerbate my incontinence.

In fact, it was not until I left home at the age of fifteen to attend boarding school that I finally outgrew this annoying phase of my life. I had been at the boarding school for several months before I realized that my bed-wetting problem had totally disappeared. No longer was I faced with disapproval, taunts, and ridicule. No one there had been informed of my childhood vexation, so no one knew! What freedom! What release I had experienced there!

This realization was to me a sure indication that my incontinence, though possibly brought on by my childhood loss of innocence, was perpetuated to such unusual lengths at home because of my feelings of open derision and shame.

The occasional taunting I experienced as a small child had escalated into what might be considered emotional abuse, as in the public humiliation of receiving a wet-diapered toddler's birthday card for my twelfth birthday.

The night I turned six and my birthday cake blew up under the engineering expertise of my father, I truly believe something snapped inside of me. Had he shown remorse, I believe I could have handled it, or gotten over it. But regardless of my tears and obvious trauma, he seemed to really have enjoyed the entertainment. I mistakenly perceived my suffering to be entertainment to him.

From that time on, I had a fear of firecrackers, motorcycles, loud mufflers, and guns; all the things that real boys and men were made of, so I thought. As I turned my attentions to the finer things of life, such as music, cooking, and crocheting, I then became a sissy in the eyes of some of the masculine gender. My recognition of their perception of me only served to widen the gap of estrangement I sensed to the male side of the family and to their macho friends.

My father's besetting sin of giving way to his wrath when disciplining his children, not only me, placed him in the category of being somewhat physically abusive, though in actuality it was quite rare. He eventually came to grips with this fault and acknowledges it today. However, the effect of his physical abuse toward me resulted in only worsening my already existing emotional stress and confusion. It was a contributing factor, along with all the others, of course, to my developing a type of fear toward men.

In many respects, "real" boys and men became the opposite sex, because I did not fit in with them and didn't really feel accepted by them. I never felt that I could measure up, fit in, nor meet with their approval.

In my self-examination, I began to see that my obsession with looking neat and attractive, or "looking good," was actually an indication of my great need for approval and acceptance and recognition. This trait was greatly misunderstood by my father, which only led to more episodes of emotional abuse.

Along with my fear and sense of inadequacy came a longing for association with certain ones of this "opposite sex" that developed into fantasies. The fantasies were innocent at first, fantasies of just being close friends and pals, being wanted. These fantasies became perverted into romantic fantasies, which eventually became even more warped and perverted into sexual fantasies.

The resulting guilt made it very difficult for me to feel comfortable around good-looking, athletic boys. I felt attracted, yet intimidated. And I feared they could see lust in my eyes if ever they looked, so I had a very difficult time looking them in the eyes. (Actually, I had difficulty looking anyone in the eyes, for fear they could see into the windows of my soul). This made me uncomfortable and awkward around certain males, and I really became a pitiful specimen of boyhood and manhood in my own estimation.

My feelings toward men, I truly believe, developed as those of a girl would develop toward men. Girls are not generally attracted to just any and every man, as any intelligent person would acknowledge. And neither was I. But every once in a while, someone would come along that just left me in a miserable state of longing.

*   *   *   *   *

With years of these thoughts and fantasies in my mind, by the time I learned of "the birds and the bees," I really was not very interested in the natural function of things. Girls were pretty. Girls were fun. Girls I dated. But girls were not the primary object of my sexual attraction as I entered puberty and grew to manhood.

Of course, everyone knew that all normal boys were attracted to girls, and, therefore, I attempted to be normal in that way. Indeed, I did have girl friends at times. I remember writing notes back and forth in grade school; the first thrill of holding a little girl's hand in an attempt at romance; my first kiss when I was sixteen; and my high school sweetheart who ended up breaking my heart. But during all those years of attempting to have normal romantic relationships with girls, there was always this festering undercurrent of love and lust for their *brothers* or other good-looking high school and college boys!

After years of conditioning, when unexpectedly faced with the episodes of uninvited advances, experimentation and exploration into the world of sexuality by an older schoolmate, I was a prime and vulnerable target. No matter what my belief system was, I had allowed my inner cravings and longings to leave me defenseless.

Where was God at that time? I don't know! I never called out to Him for strength or intervention. He was not invited. I *chose* to allow the escapade to be repeated and to escalate to the point of getting totally out of hand. And, once introduced, I then fell into the practice of occasional secret self-abuse.

The feelings of guilt that flooded over me were almost overwhelming, and I would *promise* God that I would never, never do it again. Yes, my covenant with the Lord was no better than that old covenant of ancient Israel. I would hold out for a long time, only to eventually have another, and yet another moral fall. I had become sexually active; and my self-abuse was, more often than not, involved with homosexual romantic fantasies involving fictional super heroes, movie stars, great athletes, and even men I knew from school and church. This only served to consistently reinforce in my mind the inevitable.

"As the twig is bent, so grows the tree. . . ."

*   *   *   *   *

At this juncture, I am reminded of the huge number of arguments produced by my brothers and sisters in the gay activist community in favor of the idea that sexual orientation is not changeable. While my own personal self-analysis has convinced me that my bent was environmentally conditioned, more than a third of gays now believe they were *born* that way, a 400 percent increase in fifty years.[1] Consequently, they are convinced that homosexuals are incapable of changing or of being changed.

I respect their belief, for it was my own for many years. In fact, I accept that as long as this belief is held, it might as well be factual with those who hold to it, for perception is reality in the mind of the perceiver. There is much scientific evidence, however, to substantiate the theory that homosexual orientation and behavior is a learned behavior.[2]

Nevertheless, as a homosexual myself, I had dismissed such ridiculous scientific claims as nonsense, for "they obviously were researched with a bias by heterosexuals with an anti-gay agenda, having no way of understanding my mind, feelings, and emotions," I thought.

But being born homosexual, choosing to be so, or being environmentally conditioned to be one is not the issue that should really be of concern. Rather, how can the homosexual be aroused to his need, if there is one; and how can that *need* be met, regardless of how and why he happens to be what he is? Do we just accept homosexuality in ourselves or in others as an acceptable alternate lifestyle, or do we see a need for redirection, and a means to accomplish that end? Is the issue of homosexuality a salvation issue, or is it a non-issue? Is it an eternal reality issue? Did Jesus come to save the homosexual *in* his homosexuality, or *from* his homosexuality? (Mat. 1:21).

Notes

1. Cameron, P., *Exposing the AIDS Scandal* (Lafayette, LA: Huntington House Publishers, 1988).

2. Whitehead, Neil and Briar, *My Genes Made Me Do It!* (Lafayette, LA: Huntington House Publishers, 1999).

Nineteen

A Close and Honest Look at Myself . . . Finally

Continuing in my self-scrutiny, I ventured further to take a close and honest look at myself, finally, as one living the active homosexual lifestyle.

Since entering the "gay" life in my mid twenties, I had had two long term monogamous relationships, was now in my third with numerous encounters in between. Though we never went through an actual ceremony in these long-term relationships, we did commit to one another for life, and we lived as if we were married; that is, until we got tired of each other, or thought we could upgrade to an even better "Mr. Right."

In light of my religious upbringing and belief system, I was always weighed down by the burden of guilt for my lifestyle. But not knowing how to deal with this guilt, it was easy for me to cast all the blame on God, not only for my homosexuality, but also for the progressive difficulties I was experiencing.

My life was out of control. Living the "gay" life in southern California I had busied myself not only with work, hobbies and non-competitive sports, but also with empty pleasures, parties, drinking, smoking, drugs, night club friends that really didn't know me at all, shallow relationships, and three deeply committed "marriages," including the then-present relationship.

The "gay" life also meant for me a double life. In the business world, I tried to appear to be like everyone else. Of course, I could not pretend to be married, but I did enjoy bragging about my children and having their pictures on display. I operated under the pretense of being a divorcee bachelor with on again, off again room mates. When a girl friend (a friend who just happened to be a girl), decided at one point to move in with "us," it was very convenient for me, helping to confuse the inquisitive and to uphold the lie I was living in some circles. The intended impression was that all three of us were nothing more than roommates.

Living this kind of a lie posed many problems for me, because a single man frequently becomes the object of some lady's interest, especially a well-groomed, physically fit, single man who has cultivated for a lifetime his desire to be admired, accepted, approved, and respected. When I could not produce evidence of a girl friend, then I was hard pressed to give an acceptable explanation as to why I was just simply not interested in a certain lady's attentions without offending her.

Perhaps it would have been easier to just come out of the closet, but I must admit, I was ashamed of who and what I *really* was. My long history of wanting to be liked and respected left me ill-equipped to handle well the inevitable disapproval and ridicule of others toward homosexuals.

Outside influences and complications were beginning to threaten what had seemed to be a perfect life with Andy. Careerwise, I had begun a new venture in business with a fellow salesman. He was president, and I was vice president of a new corporation. We were having to put almost everything we made back into the company to really get it going, which meant greatly reduced take-home pay for both of us.

Meeting my own personal monthly financial obligations had become an ever-increasing challenge. Rent was very high in southern California, and I was having more and more difficulty paying my share. I got behind on my car payments, and eventually it was repossessed. My credit cards were close to their limits, and I could no longer keep up with the minimum payments, resulting in judgments filed against me.

The business looked as though it was really going to take off, so I hung in with it to my own personal financial collapse. The courts had raised my child support payments to over one third of my gross income. Trying to juggle all my financial obligations left me seriously behind in all of them.

The District Attorney's office had messed up their book-keeping on my child support account and was coming down hard on me for not being able to keep up with the child support. Yes, I was behind, but not as much as their records were indicating.

My son was to graduate from eighth grade in a couple weeks, so I offered to go up to northern California at that time for a hearing to resolve our dispute. On the way I called to verify the time and place of my appointment. The clerk, looking over my file, advised me that I was to report to the jail, not the court house.

"What?" I reacted. "I was told that I could have a hearing and get this resolved."

"No, sir," she responded. "You are to report to the jail. There is a warrant for your arrest, and if you show up at the court house, you will just be arrested and taken to jail anyway. So, please report to the jail."

"Thank you, ma'am," I snapped, then hung up.

What a dilemma I was now facing! Andy was traveling with me, and I told him what was happening. "This whole thing is a set up," I said. "They lied to me! They acted like they were interested in working together to resolve this mess, and all they intended to do was throw me in jail! I would then miss my son's graduation, and how would I explain that to him. Besides, he's counting on wearing one of my party suits for his graduation! Andy," I announced decisively, "we're going straight to the graduation. Forget the DA's office for now. I'll handle that later. We can not miss this graduation."

We arrived at the school several hours later.

"Dad!" Donnie greeted me with his big, winning smile. "You made it! Did you bring that suit I asked to borrow?"

After a big bear hug, I gave him the suit and he disappeared into the restroom to change. Andy and I sat near the back of the auditorium with my daughter. With great pride, I watched my little man child (not so little anymore. He could wear my clothes ...), as he marched down the aisle to the processional. After the preliminaries, it was announced that the young people would now take roses to their parents in the audience. Just at that moment, I felt a tap on my shoulder. Turning around I faced Leanne.

"Jesse," she said soberly. "I got a call from the DA's office just before leaving home. They wanted to know if you were planning on being here for Donnie's graduation, and I told them you were. They then said they were on their way over to arrest you; something about you not appearing in court today?"

I thanked her for the information, then turned to Andy. "We've got to get out of here," I whispered. "The cops are coming to get me!"

Turning to my daughter I said, "Stephanie, honey. An emergency has arisen, and I can't stay. Please tell Donnie that I'll call him tonight after the ceremony. I'll explain everything to you both then. I'm sorry, honey. I have to go."

She just looked at me with wonder and confusion, not knowing what to say. I hugged her, and Andy and I slipped out the back as Donnie was coming down the aisle with my rose. Looking at my empty seat next to his sister, "Where's Dad?" he asked.

"I don't know. He said he had to go. There was some kind of emergency, and he said he'd call us at Mom's after the ceremony."

Donnie gave my rose to his sister and, confused, walked back up to the platform.

A few moments later, Andy and I were in a local bar. I needed a drink; a stiff one. No, I needed two; or was it three? How could this have happened to me? How could I have done this to my son? I was so filled with remorse and despair. Then thinking of the DA's office, I got angry. They were going to pay for this! I determined to fight them from that day on.

Later that night I called the children from a motel and explained what had happened, hoping they could understand. But all the understanding in the world could not erase the disappointment of the evening spoiled.

Arriving home the next day, I told Andy that I needed to go back and get this thing resolved with the DA. He let me

borrow his car, and eight hours later I was in the courthouse.
I told the clerk who I was and who I wanted to see, that I was
there for a hearing to resolve a dispute. She looked at me with
surprise and not a little disdain. I wasn't used to this kind of
reaction to my presence, and I didn't like it one bit.

She excused herself to make a quick phone call. I noticed
the cold stares of the other office workers and wondered why
they all looked at me with such foreboding. It was just me,
Jesse, come to work out our dispute. To them, I was a wanted
criminal. The clerk returned and told me I was to have gone to
the other court house. Thereupon I turned to go.

"No!" she snapped. "Just wait right here! They're coming
over here to talk to you."

"But I can just go over there, can't I?"

"No!" she snapped again coldly. "You are to wait right
here."

Minutes later, policemen bolted through all the entrances
and exits and I was arrested as if on their ten most wanted list.

"Put your hands over your head!" one of them barked at
me.

They then frisked me, cuffed my hands behind my back,
and started berating me loudly in front of everyone. Obviously,
they wanted to make an example out of me, and they really
enjoyed this opportunity to play "cops."

Hurrying me out the door, they stuffed me into the back
seat of a squad car and drove me to the front of the county
court house. The district attorney was just walking out, and
they called him over.

"We caught the son of a b——!" they bragged. I could see
that I was brownie points for them.

"You didn't catch me, you jerks!" I muttered under my
breath. "I came here of my own free will. Cowards! Liars!" I
called them a few other names as well, but I won't elaborate.

From there they took me to jail. Hours later I was ushered
into court, handcuffed, and humiliated. Painfully, I listened to
all the trumped up charges against me, not being allowed to
answer for myself. I was then ordered to be returned to jail to
await trial scheduled for two weeks later.

"Two weeks!" I reacted to myself. "I'm up here in a borrowed car that will no doubt end up being towed. I was told to come for a hearing! They lied to me! They never intended to sit down and talk with me. They lied! If I ever get out of this place, they'll never see any cooperation out of me again, ever!"

Back in jail, the officer in charge asked me what I was in for. I explained as briefly as possible what had happened. He looked at me for a moment. Stamped a piece of paper and said, "Get outta here."

"What?" I asked in disbelief,

"Get outta here. My jail is overcrowded, and I have the authority to let one person go. Sounds to me like you shouldn't be in here anyway. Go on, get outta here."

"But, my car is on the other side of town. I have no money on me for a phone call or a cab. Can I get a ride?" I can't believe I did that.

"Friend, all I can do is open the door. You wanna go, or ya wanna stay?"

"Thanks," I said. "I'll go."

"Make sure you show up in court in two weeks," he warned as I hurried out the door.

I had to walk across town and hunt for the other courthouse and the car. Then I hightailed it out of that county as fast as I could go without getting pulled over. Man! Was I ever mad! "Who do those jerks think they are that they can play with someone's life like this?" I yelled.

Two weeks later I was back in court. A court appointed lawyer had been assigned to me, and it turned out that he went to church with my ex-wife and knew her well. He turned out to be my worst enemy; hardly what I would ever expect in an advocate. I watched him work as the public defender. Every case that was called up, he had the accused plead either "no contest" or "guilty."

"What kind of a boob is this guy anyway?" I wondered.

During a break, he called me outside to talk. Showing me pictures of the nice house I lived in (they had spied on me), he asked if that was where I lived, never thinking that I could just be renting a room in it.

"Yes."

"Is this your car out front?" pointing to a nice BMW that belonged to a friend of my room mate.

"No."

"Do you think you can convince this court of that?"

"I don't have to" I smarted off. "They have to prove that it is!"

"Are you going to plead guilty to the charges against you here?"

"No! Of course not. I came to settle a dispute. Their records are wrong, and I can prove it!"

Grabbing my necktie and pulling it up behind my left ear, "You're just going to hang yourself. I can't win this case for you."

"How about if I write everything out for you, and you just get up and read it, okay?" I sneered at him. I couldn't believe this wimp was representing me in court.

He turned and stomped back into the courtroom.

When my name was called, the prosecutor was surprised to see me come forward on my own, dressed sharply with a tie instead of an orange monkey suit and being ushered in handcuffed by a deputy. They had me thrown in jail two weeks earlier, and, obviously, until this moment had not known I was out.

The charges were read against me, but I pleaded, "Not guilty, your honor!" The first such plea of the entire day. There was a bit of confusion, then the judge asked if he could meet with all of us in his chambers: the prosecutor, the investigator who had taken such pride in capturing this criminal at large, the District Attorney, and my court appointed excuse for an advocate.

In his private chambers, the judge asked for an explanation. When all was said and done against me, my own lawyer being the most vocal, the judge then asked if I had anything to say. Finally! I shared with him my documentation, much to the surprise of my opponents. My own lawyer had never even taken the time to listen to me and see that I might just be in the right. I also revealed to them in the presence of the judge that I had discovered in my research for defense that for every $1.00 of child support they collected, they received over $3.00 in federal funds for collecting it. I was on to them, and they did not like it!

The judge pronounced, "Gentlemen, it seems to me that this should not be a case in court, but that you ought to get your records straight. This gentleman seems to have very well documented his payments, and I suggest you amend your records and all work together on this in the future. Young man, you are free to go!"

If looks could kill! And they were mutual. Wow! It felt so good to be vindicated in the presence of my enemies.

From that day on, however, I was on their list. A war was raging that would go on for years. I initiated court action, representing myself, to get my child support reduced commensurate with my income. The court ruled again in my favor. I had won another victory, but it was a shallow one, because my financial situation was on the verge of total collapse. It was difficult for me to even keep up with the reduced rate.

*   *   *   *   *

Another factor working to pull me down was the decision Andy and I had made, while once under the influence of alcohol, to invite others to enter into our sexual relationship. It seemed to be an exciting adventure at first, but I soon regretted this intrusion into our private life. The ensuing extramarital activities, though few, worked against us, weakening the bond that we had created, resulting in jealousy and suspicion that served to undermine our relationship.

As time went on, my worsening state of existence only escalated. Andy was now having to carry much more than his load financially. I just could not seem to get out of my downward spiral financially, then emotionally. Once again, I was seized with panic, anxiety, which was probably nothing less than depression. I finally hit bottom financially, and in my depression was becoming totally dependent. It was here that the Lord could finally get my attention. He brought me to my knees. I had nowhere else to go. I was to the point where I despised myself and all that I had become. It no longer mattered how I had gotten here. Years of blaming God and blaming others had not prevented me from ending up in this state of total desperation.

I was reaping that which God had declared to be the result of a course of sin,

> a trembling heart, and failing of eyes, and sorrow of mind: and thy life shall hang in doubt before thee; and thou shalt fear day and night, and shalt have none assurance of thy life: in the morning thou shalt say, Would God it were even! And at even thou shalt say, Would God it were morning! For the fear of thine heart wherewith thou shalt fear, and for the sight of thine eyes which thou shalt see. (Deut. 28:65-67)

As a sinner, my own thoughts were my accusers, and there can be no torture keener than the stings of a guilty conscience, which gave me no rest day nor night.

Finally! I had taken a close and honest look at myself in my present condition. It was so painful. How I detested what I saw in myself. Though I truly loved Andy, and he truly loved me, I began to realize my need of deliverance from this life of degradation. I was drowning in a sea of wickedness and despair. I needed a lifeguard!

Twenty

"My Son, Give Me Thine Heart"

My parents were unable to visit me very often since they lived on the other side of the country. However, whenever they did come, I was always blessed by their company. Their seemingly uncomplicated, simple lifestyle was very refreshing to me. I would chuckle in amusement when traveling with them, for they would notice and remark about the most insignificant things along the byways. My life was in the fast lane, and I had no time to "stop and smell the roses." But they seemed to appreciate the most insignificant little things. I longed for that simplicity to be in my own life once again.

Whenever they were with me they wanted me to take them to church, of course, and I would usually humor them. I knew what they were doing, but that was all right. They were gently attempting to nudge me in the right direction, but without preaching at me.

My mother loves nature. One day, I took them to the Botanical Gardens near where I lived. Now, I could have been in and out of that place and seen everything in one-third the time that it took for them. They marveled at every little detail.

My mother was the worst! Dad and I could not walk slowly enough to keep up with her. Stopping in the shade of a tree, we waited for her to catch up. As we saw her finally approaching, we noticed the radiant smile on her face. She was thoroughly enjoying this outing in the garden. As she got closer we noticed something even more on her face. Totally unaware of it herself, the end of her nose was completely powdered with a bright yellow substance, to the entertainment of others walking in the garden.

"Oh, Honey!" approaching she exclaimed to Dad, oblivious to her yellow nose. "You should have smelled those big flowers right back there. They were heavenly."

We burst out laughing, for she was truly a comical sight.

"What's the matter?" she asked, blushing with embarrassment, and unwittingly joining in with our laughter.

"That's my Mamasita!" grinned Dad as he grabbed her and gave her a squeeze. There was something reassuring to me, and all my siblings, about the way Dad had always played and even flirted with his wife, our mother. No one ever doubted that he was very much in love with her, for he was very open with affection toward her.

"Mom, your nose is coated with yellow pollen!" I laughed. "You truly do have to 'stop and smell the roses,' don't you?"

Understanding now the smiles and chuckles of passersby, blushing beet red, yet thoroughly amused with herself, she laughed uncontrollably as she quickly wiped at her nose with one of her ever-present tissues.

It was with mixed feelings that I bade them farewell upon their eventual departure. Their loving bond with each other was a stability factor in my own capricious life. More and more I realized how much I depended upon their existence for my own security. One part of me longed for their constant companionship, while the other part of me was craving getting back to my life of pleasure and vice.

Invariably, after their departure I would find lying around the house somewhere a token of their visit. A booklet, perhaps, or a magazine, or a tract would be left on the coffee table, in my book case, or even under my pillow. These I collected over the years, never able to discard them. They were gifts of love.

My parents knew it was futile to attempt talking to me about religion. I was just not interested. However, their unconditional love and acceptance over the years worked to break down the barriers.

As I had continued my process of self-analysis, prompted repeatedly by those recurring dreams, a nagging longing began developing within me for a spiritual dimension in my life. With this longing there awoke within me a desire to study out some of the issues that had come to my mind. Only a small desire at first, it began to grow stronger.

Somewhere I found an old Bible, and I tried to read it. But it really didn't hold my interest. My taste for the spiritual, especially the concentrated word of the Bible, was seriously lacking.

Soon I found myself pulling out some of those little tokens of my parents visits and browsing through them. I remember deciding to examine one of their books one day; but first I fixed myself a nice, big, icy margarita. Then I sat down with that margarita in one hand, lit up a cigarette with the other, and commenced reading a little book called *Finding Peace Within*. About this time, I realized how ludicrous this little scene must look to God above, so I spoke a brief word to Him.

"God, this cigarette and this margarita are the least of the problems in my life right now, as You must certainly know. I'm just checking to see what kind of answers you might have for the big ones. If I see something worthwhile, then we can deal with these *little* vices later."

And, so I read on. The book was beautiful. On the very first page I read, "Nature and revelation alike testify of God's love. . . . The world, though fallen, is not all sorrow and misery. In nature itself are messages of hope and comfort. There are flowers upon the thistles, and the thorns are covered with roses."

What an outlook on life this author had. And, surely, this is what I needed: messages of hope and comfort, for my life was truly one of despair.

I was still smoking and nursing a margarita when I got into chapter five. Here I read,

> God does not require us to give up anything that it is for
> our best interest to retain. In all that He does, He has
> the well-being of His children in view. Would that all
> who have not chosen Christ might realize that He has

> something vastly better to offer them than they are seek-
> ing for themselves. No real joy can be found in the path
> forbidden by Him who knows what is best, and who
> plans for the good of His creatures. The path of trans-
> gression is the path of misery and destruction. (*Finding
> Peace Within*, 37)

"The path forbidden by Him who knows what is best . . ."
I repeated softly.

Would that forbidden path include my gay lifestyle over
which I seem to have no choice or control? I mused.

I reached over and snuffed out my cigarette, realizing there
was no excuse for my indulgence. "Wow! I've had this thing
about God all wrong! I've been blaming Him all these years for
the pain and sorrow and misery that I have really just brought
upon myself by my stubborn resistance against His perfect will
for my peace and happiness. But this makes sense. Surely 'Father' does know best for the children of His own creation."

At this point I was hooked. I could see a little flicker of
light at the end of my tunnel. I had to study further and get to
the bottom of all my questions. Though I had difficulty reading the Bible, I soon was staying up, sometimes until 2:00 in
the morning, reading this book and another one about the
history of the great controversy between Christ and Satan that
began in heaven and would eventually end here on earth. I was
completely unaware of it, but my taste for the spiritual was
being very thoroughly cultivated, because the author of these
books was guilty of "plagiarizing" other authors, such as Matthew, Mark, Luke, and John, Isaiah, and Moses. I could hardly
read a single page of these two books without becoming immersed in Scripture; for there were beautiful quotations, precious gems of thought on virtually every page, directly from the
Bible.

It wasn't long before I was able to read the Bible with
enjoyment, for hours at a time. The lesser light of these other
books was cultivating within me an appetite for the greater
light of the Bible itself.

One day I decided to visit a church in the greater Los
Angeles area. A business client of mine had invited me, and I

thought it would at least be an interesting change of pace. To my discomfort, the sermon that day happened to be on the destruction of Sodom and Gomorrah! I felt increasingly uneasy, especially knowing personally six other homosexuals sitting in this same congregation. Five of them, including my client, were active members in this church. So I wondered where the minister might be going with his sermon. Never once did he speak of homosexuality, neither in the narrative of the story nor in the body of his sermon. It was never named as one of the sins of Sodom, neither was it named as a sin at all. Rather, he concluded the sin of Sodom and Gomorrah to be the sin of inhospitality!

"What?" I reacted in silent shock and amazement. "Inhospitality! I'm a homosexual, and I know better than that!"

My recent study of the Bible had clearly shown me,

> Behold, this was the iniquity of thy sister Sodom, pride, fullness of bread, and abundance of idleness was in her and in her daughters, neither did she strengthen the hand of the poor and needy. And they were haughty, and committed *abomination* before me: therefore I took them away as I saw good. (Ezek. 16:49-50)

The account of the destruction of Sodom in Genesis 18 and 19 detailed the abominable efforts of the men of the city to "know" (in the Biblical sense, to lie with) the men [angels] visiting in the home of Lot, to which Lot reacted by offering his daughters. This strange act, of course, was not a righteous one either.

Homosexuality is one of many sins[1] clearly listed Biblically as abominations: "If a man also lie with mankind, as he lieth with a woman, both of them have committed an abomination" (Lev. 18:22; 20:13).

I left that church realizing that I might be made to feel comfortable there with my homosexuality, but not comfortable that I was hearing the truth of the matter. And I would really like to know the truth, the whole truth, and nothing but the truth while there is still time to be reproved, corrected, and instructed, and not discover the truth when it is too late.

I had by now been living the "gay" life for about fifteen years. One day while at work a business associate of mine discovered through our conversation that I had once been a Christian of the same denomination with which he was now affiliated, and he invited me to visit his church sometime.

A few weeks later I did just that, out of curiosity more than anything else. As a businessman, I had several nice suits hanging in my closet, and I knew that wearing my best was really only appropriate for church. But I chose not to wear one. Instead, I purposely selected attire not appropriate for church; clothes that would say, "I'm not a member here. I'm not one of you people." In fact, I dressed as if going to "happy hour" at a gay bar. Perhaps I had a subconscious desire to draw attention to myself as a visitor; maybe deep down inside I was crying out for help and wanted someone to recognize that I was of the world, a person in spiritual need.

As I entered the church attended by about 5000 people, I thought to myself, "My! This church is full of visitors!"

To my surprise, after looking around the congregation, I realized I did *not* stand out in the crowd as a visitor. The church was extremely liberal. There was nothing about the appearance of these people that would indicate to me that they were of the kingdom "not of this world," and I was somewhat put off by the outward display in a body of people calling themselves Christians, though it didn't bother me at all to see it in people of the world. I myself was a prime example of that.

In my reading, I had learned of a couple of young reformers centuries earlier who had attempted to make a point of comparison between the pompous image of the bishop of Rome and the humility of Jesus Christ. They had painted a picture on the side of a building depicting the meek and lowly Jesus riding on a little donkey contrasted with one of the pontiff with all his regal attire and entourage. The picture was surely worth a thousand words. It stuck in my mind.

I sat through the entire service in shock as I listened to the rock 'n' roll band and the lead singers on stage. I had been involved in worldly dancing for fifteen years, and the music, rather than reaching my heart, reached instead my happy feet

which wanted to get up and dance. It did not lift my thoughts
heavenward, but rather drove them back to associations with
night clubs and dance halls I had frequented all those years.
Church, I thought, should be a sanctuary from the din and
clamor of the world, not a reinforcement of that which I needed
to escape.

I watched the mood of the congregation being manipulated by the lighting and the music to where many were react-
ing with reckless abandon, not unlike what happens at the rock
concerts and in the theaters that I had frequented over the past
fifteen years. One might say these people "had the spirit." And
that may have been so, however 1 John 4:1-3 counsels us to try
the spirits, or test them, whether they are of God. Evidently
there are spirits that cannot be trusted.

My reading had led me to the text in Isaiah 8:20 that
directs us to the only safe test in religious matters, "To the law
and to the testimony: if they speak not according to this word,
it is because there is no light in them." The Word of God
should be the Christian's only rule of faith and practice. Feelings and emotions are, no doubt, very much a part of having a
relationship with God. But they are not safe tests of what is
right and wrong. Feelings and emotions can get people into a
lot of trouble. Ask me! Fifteen years of riotous living were the
result of my allowing feelings and emotions to be my rule of
life rather than the Word of God. The emotional manipula-
tion in that service really disturbed me.

A drama was later acted out on stage conducted by a hired
thespian from the Screen Actors Guild in Hollywood as I was
later informed.

"This was not church," I mused. "This was theater!"

As I sat through the service, I remember tears welling up
into my eyes as I inquired under my breath, "God, what have
they done to your church?"

"What have you been doing these past fifteen years to
counteract it?" came His quick reply by an impression in my
mind.

Instead of condemnation toward the church, I realized
shame and remorse within myself. Yes, I had been trained to

be a minister of the gospel. What *one thing* had I done in the last fifteen years to the glory of God? Nothing!

I left that church feeling a little kick in the pants. There was a character in the Bible I could relate to whose name was Jonah. I had been a long-term Jonah! It had taken only three days to bring him to his spiritual senses. And me? Fifteen years? The Lord was really laying one on me!

Not one person spoke to me after the service. No one knew I was a visitor nor seemed to care. But then, I thought, when leaving theaters of entertainment I never expect anyone to come up to me and introduce himself and invite me to dinner or to a study group. This was very much the same as leaving a theater. Everyone seemed to just find his way to his own car and leave.

I remember my feelings of despondence upon driving out of the parking lot. Actually, it was like leaving a restaurant after eating only the salad (no dressing). I felt unfed, unsatisfied, un-nourished. I also began to realize a sense of calling to share the principles I was discovering in my own personal study.

At home, I continued studying, hours upon hours at a time. It seemed that light began to just pour in upon me through the word of God, and I wanted to respond, but did not yet know how. "What happened to me fifteen years ago that left me without hope and left me outside the Christian church?" I again acknowledged that God surely could not have been at fault. The fault had to somehow lie with me. But how? I really thought I had made all the right choices against my inclinations, but fell from grace nonetheless.

Through a series of revival meetings I happened upon, I began reading the Bible more in order to follow along with what was being presented. Like the Bereans of old, I "received the word with all readiness of mind, and searched the Scriptures daily whether those things were so."

The Holy Spirit was really working on my heart, giving me no rest day nor night. In the words of Solomon, He was calling out to me, "My son, give me thine heart, and let thine eyes observe my ways" (Prov. 23:26). I later learned that through the intercessory prayers of my parents, the Holy Spirit was being asked specifically to do that very thing; to give me no rest day nor night.

As I continued to behold Christ in my study of His word, I began seeing more clearly the awfulness of sin, and to realize in particular the awfulness of my own life of sin. The desire welled up inside me to be set free. My lifestyle was not in harmony with the will of my Creator, else why would I keep having those recurring dreams that left me feeling the horror of being lost; why the ever growing sense of guilt? Not only would I have been out of place in Eden, I knew in my heart that I would not feel at home in heaven either, facing my Creator.

*   *   *   *   *

In another church I visited, the guest speaker was a very prominent theologian from a very prominent seminary. I was impressed by his presentation until about midway when he made a statement that startled me. "We will be sinning right up until the time that Jesus comes to take us home."

"What?" I reacted in my mind. "Did I hear this man correctly?"

I couldn't believe my ears. For someone like me who had enjoyed the pleasures of a sinful life for a fifteen year season, for someone who now wanted desperately to be set free from that bondage—that lifestyle, the idea that we will be sinning until Jesus returns was a devastating blow. Where was the hope? I was not wanting to be saved in my lifestyle of sin. I desperately needed and wanted to be saved *from* sin itself, *from* homosexuality. Waiting for Jesus to come was not soon enough for me. I had followed a downward spiral of self-destruction, and I now needed a Savior who could rescue me from myself in *this* life.

And "What about the text in Revelation 22:11," I thought, "that says, 'He that is unjust, let him be unjust still: and he which is filthy, let him be filthy still: and he that is righteous, let him be righteous still: and he that is holy, let him be holy still.'?"

"What sinning can I continue to do and still be received into heaven? How much sinning can I get away with, and still make it there? Does he really believe that I can continue my homosexual lifestyle and be accepted into heaven?" I queried.

In visiting various churches around the greater Los Angeles area, I found myself deeply disappointed. Instead of finding answers on how to be set free from a life of sin, I kept hearing week after week, from one church to another, that we will be sinning until Christ returns, then we will be changed and sin will be no more. It seemed as if everywhere I turned I was being told that it was impossible for me to live a life free from sin, which to me meant that it was impossible for me to overcome my homosexual lifestyle completely. I wondered if they knew that their teaching was offering no hope whatsoever to someone such as I, and that it was in essence offering a Christian license to homosexual behavior.

In church study groups I began to get myself into a little trouble when expressing my *sincere* questions and observations. My study was showing me that I could change, that I could *be* changed. Jesus came to save His people *from* their sins, not *in* their sins. These principles I began to share in church discussion groups, not experientially as yet but at least the good news of the promises of salvation *from* sin, the theory of the gospel. And in sharing with these classes, I was hoping to receive some confirmation. If I was going to attempt a change in lifestyle, I needed assurance that it was not going to be an exercise in futility.

One teacher came to me after his class one day, introduced himself, and then said, "You know, Jesse, I've been a pastor for forty years, and I've never met a perfect person yet!"

"My!" I thought. "What a sad testimony to your ministry. First of all, how would you know one if you saw one? The only thing you know about me is my name. How do you know that I have not achieved perfection of character? (Of course I was not claiming that for myself.) And who are you to judge anyway? Furthermore, I doubt that you have been preaching 'victory over sin,' so you need not ever expect to see it."

In one book I was reading, I came across a statement that really had the ring of truth to it,

> In every phase of your character building you are to
> please God. This you may do: for Enoch pleased Him
> though living in a degenerate age. And there are Enochs
> in this our day.[2]

And why not? The Bible was full of examples of godly
men such as Enoch who had by faith in Jesus overcome sin
(Heb. 11, the faith chapter).

I was terribly disappointed by this minister's lack of faith.
Just when I was beginning to see hope for myself that Jesus
could save me from my sin of homosexuality, I was being shot
down. This preacher was telling me that he did not believe in
victory over sin. My only solace was in my own continued
personal study. I decided to become a "Berean" as mentioned
in Acts 17:11, and to receive the Word with all readiness of
mind, and to search the Scriptures daily, to determine for myself whether those things were so.

What blessed things I discovered! I began to realize what
had happened to me 15 years earlier when I had left the Christian church with no hope. I had not wanted to fall into the life
of sin that was about to devour me. I was going through my
own Garden of Gethsemane experience, but did not know how
to live by faith. I did not understand these things about Jesus
that would have assured me of His empathy. I did know that
the direction I was heading would separate me from God and
eternal life, but I had become a victim of a serious error in
theology that was prevalent then and is still today, teaching
that we cannot have victory over sin until Jesus returns.

But, honestly, this makes no sense! If we have no hope of
overcoming sin completely but will be sinning until Christ
returns, then why must one *not* just every once in awhile commit murder, not every day, but maybe just once a year? or steal,
or commit adultery, or have a homosexual encounter?

If we will be sinning until the return of Christ, then how
can one look at the homosexual and encourage a change of
lifestyle, or suggest that change is even necessary, for whatever
reason?

Is there a value attached to sin making one sin acceptable, or excusable by God until Christ returns, while another one is not permissible?

On another occasion, I was invited out after church by a family to participate in an activity that was in direct violation of Christian principles. Over dinner, they asked me if the Lord was giving me victory over my smoking. I answered in the negative.

"Now, why," I asked myself, "are they concerned over my sinful practices and not concerned over their own?"

It began to occur to me that with many Christians there must be two classifications of sins: those which are socially acceptable, and those which are socially *un*acceptable. I, evidently, was a socially *un*acceptable sinner within many Christian circles, so it was necessary for me to reform my behavior by their standards. But, evidently, should one's sins be socially acceptable, he might continue falling occasionally right up until the second coming of Christ and be saved anyway! Only this is inconsistent and unbiblical Christian behavior and theology!"

If sin is defined as "the transgression of the law" (1 John 3:4), I reasoned, then which one of God's ten commandments are we allowed to practice breaking until Jesus comes? For the white-liar and the perjurer it is the ninth one. For the kleptomaniac, robber, thief, and extortioner it is the eighth one. For the golly gee and the outright profane it is the third one. For the pre- and extramarital sex offender, the pornographer, the divorcee in many cases, the child molester, the self-abuser, and the homosexual, all are guilty of the same sin as defined in the seventh commandment. For the forgetful, it is the fourth commandment.

Can the murderer continue to fall into sin until Jesus comes and be assured of salvation? As the apostle Paul puts it, "What shall we say then? Shall we continue in sin, that grace may abound? God forbid" (Rom. 6:1).

To excuse sin of any kind is most assuredly faulty reasoning, for the Scriptures tell us that if we offend in *one point*, we are guilty of them all (James 2:10).

Furthermore, in my study I could not find one text of scripture that left me comfortable with the teaching that I could be saved *in* sin. It may be a nice idea for someone who does not want to be set free, but I was not willing to stake my hope of eternal life with our Savior on this weak premise.

However, the Bible is full of promises of salvation *from* sin; not just from the results of sin, but from sin itself.[3] For example,

> There hath no temptation taken you but such as is common to man: but God is faithful, who will not suffer you to be tempted above that ye are able; but will with the temptation also make a way to escape, that ye may be able to bear it. (1 Cor. 10:13)

A common teaching I ran up against was that "the law was nailed to the cross." This, of course, only generated more questions in my searching mind.

What law? The law that says Thou shalt not kill?, or Thou shalt not steal? and Thou shalt have no other gods before Me? Is that the law that was nailed to the cross?

If so, then why are Christians so up in arms over the crime rate in this country? If so, then why express concern over the rebellion of youth against their parents and authority in general? Why the concern over abortion, and adultery, and profanity? In teaching that the law of God is no longer binding, being nailed to the cross, does Christianity not assume some degree of responsibility for the lawlessness that is so pervasive in our society today? Does Christianity not assume some degree of responsibility for the homosexual who believes that *his* continued sin can be swept under the carpet of grace just like anyone else's besetting sin, because we are now under grace and not under the law?

As I continued to study and ponder the reasons for my own failure some fifteen years back, I was one day suddenly prompted with the thought, "Christ suffered being tempted." I felt like Martin Luther when crawling up Pilate's staircase having his impression, "The just shall live by faith."

Most of my life, I had believed that Jesus was able to live a life of perfect obedience only because He had some advantage over me, being God. I did not believe that His humanity was genuine and that He had the same struggles that I had in my humanity. This idea always gave me reason to excuse my failings, especially in the area of homosexuality. It was difficult for me to believe that even God could understand me; that He could have sympathy and compassion for me; especially in light of His calling my sin an abomination which, in the Old Testament, was to be dealt with by stoning.

I began to reason that if Christ suffered being tempted, then He surely must have had no advantage over me when it came to resisting and overcoming sin. Later I found the text, "For in that He Himself hath suffered being tempted, he is able to succor them that are tempted" (Heb. 2:18). As I came to a better understanding of the book of Hebrews, I began to develop a confidence in Jesus Christ as *my* Savior.

"Wherefore in *all* things it behoved him to be made like unto *his* brethren, that he might be a merciful and faithful high priest in things pertaining to God, to make reconciliation for the sins of the people [for the sins of the likes of myself]" (Heb. 2:17).

This text expressed perfectly the need of my soul. Perfect identity with me, not in the participation of my sin, but in being likewise tempted. Perfect identity with me was essential in order to reach me and save me from my sin. He could not function effectively as my High Priest otherwise. For I had believed Him to look upon me as an abomination, with scorn and disgust.

Reading again, "For in that he himself hath suffered being tempted, he is able to succor (aid, assist, help, relieve) them that are tempted." Only in the areas wherein He Himself had suffered being tempted could He as High Priest function effectively to relieve, or assist others like me. If I was assailed by any temptation Christ did not have to meet, in that respect I would have no Savior from that sin. Only in that He Himself had been tempted with homosexual temptation [and, mind you, temptation is not sin, nor is it sinful], only then could I as a homosexual know that He truly understood me. Then I could open up to Him and bare my soul. I now could know that He would understand; could understand even the likes of me in my state of degradation and despair.

Reading on, "For we have not an high priest which cannot be touched with the feeling of our infirmities; but was in all points tempted like as *we are, yet* without sin" (Heb. 4:15). The words in italics, I learned, were supplied for clarification by the translators. Therefore, I decided to replace the translators' supplied words in this text for further clarification for myself. The text then read, "For we have not an high priest which cannot be touched with the feeling of our infirmities; but was in all points tempted like as *Jesse is, yet* without sin. Let us, [Jesse], therefore come boldly unto the throne of grace, that we may obtain mercy, and find grace to help in time of need." That we might find that divine influence promised to work upon the heart, then to be reflected in the life, as grace is defined in Greek. That no matter how strong, how intense the temptation, you may resist it with heavenly strength and power, that heavenly influence promised to work within you to say "No! Get thee behind me, Satan!" And then allow that heavenly influence to be reflected in the life by not yielding to that temptation.

"My grace [strength, power] is sufficient for thee," Jesus says. "For my strength is made perfect in [your] weakness" (2 Cor. 12:9).

In pursuing this line of study, I began to vaguely realize the magnitude of the sacrifice Christ had made for me that I might be saved. Jesus had humbled Himself, clothing His divinity with humanity; taking upon Himself our humanity. Yes, though perfectly divine, He was also every bit as human as I, yet without sin.

The understanding that I had been cherishing all this time was that Christ had come as a second Adam, so to speak, in the nature of Adam before his fall, that it was really not possible for Him to fail; and that He thus had an advantage over me in resisting temptation to sin. I, therefore, had an excuse for never overcoming completely in that I was disadvantaged by having a sinful nature while Christ was advantaged, I thought, with a sinless nature. If, therefore, He had such an advantage, then surely a God of love would not hold me to perfect obedience, would He?

This misunderstanding of the nature of Christ had infiltrated my religious education, but its origin was with the antichrist. For the apostle John warned, "Every spirit that confesseth that Jesus Christ *is* come in the flesh (sinful nature of man) is of God: And every spirit that confesseth *not* that Jesus Christ is come in the flesh (sinful nature of man) is *not* of God, and this is that spirit of antichrist" (1 John 4:1-3).

For me to cherish the idea that it was impossible for me to live without sinning, or to stop living in sin, was nothing but an *excuse for sin*. What I now needed and desired was not an excuse for sin, but an *escape from sin*. That is an important part of what Christ's life, death, and resurrection were all about: to provide an exemplary life for us to follow, and to show us that through the Holy Spirit one can be freed from the bondage of sin. And that power through the Holy Spirit to overcome sin completely, to stop sinning, is freely given to all them that ask and are willing to accept it; willing to be changed.

This new understanding of Christ and His infinite sacrifice for me thrilled me through and through. I could now answer the question as to what had happened to me fifteen years earlier when I was going through my Gethsemane experience. *I* had failed, not God. When Christ was in the garden, He agonized all night in prayer, pleading with God that "this cup pass from Me." He sweat as it were blood. He *suffered* being tempted. But in the end, what was His prayer? "Nevertheless, *not My will, but Thine* be done."

Christ could not see through to the other side, as I could not see, yet He trusted God and surrendered His entire will to Him. That, I now realized, is living by faith, righteousness (right doing) by faith.

"Let this mind be in you, which was also in Christ Jesus: Who became obedient unto death, even the death of the cross" (Phil. 2:5-8). The mind of Jesus was completely dead to self and submissive to the will of His Father.

In my own Gethsemane experience, I had eventually given up. I did not exercise the faith in God to see me through to the other side. I expected to be freed from the suffering of *temptation*. And when I wasn't, I gave up. It was when I stopped praying for deliverance (from the desire to sin) that I actually fell into a lifestyle of sin. God had not ceased hearing and answering my prayers. I had ceased praying.

If Christ suffered being tempted, who was I to think that I should not be? Christ admonished, "Take up [your] cross, and follow Me" (Mark 8:34). In other words, "Follow My example." He never promised me a cross of no pain, no suffering, no difficulty, no *temptation*, no *self-denial*. He did promise me, however, power and strength to resist and to overcome *sin*, to not suffer me to be tempted above that I was able to endure.

"If we confess our sins, he is faithful and just to forgive us our sins, and to *cleanse us from all* unrighteousness" (1 John 1:9).

"My son, give me thine heart, and let thine eyes observe my ways." God was calling me. "My son," He says. Yes, homosexuals are God's children, too!

Notes

1. See chapter twenty-three, "You, Too, Can Be Made Whole."

2. Christ's Object Lessons, 332.

3. See chapter twenty-three, "You, Too, Can Be Made Whole."

Twenty-One

Pecking My Way Out

Somewhere I had heard the story of the eagle and its chick. When it is time for the chick to hatch out of its egg, it is crucial for its survival that it peck its own way out of the shell. This pecking goes on for some time before the actual hatching, and it works to strengthen the chick and help it mature to the point of being able to survive outside the protective environment of its shell. If the shell is opened by an overly helpful human, for example, the chick's chances of survival are greatly diminished.

Father really does know best when dealing with His children. Four years earlier, I had pleaded with the Lord to get me out of a terrible mess with a relationship gone awry. The relationship ended by mutual agreement, and we both went our separate ways. Two weeks later, I was out looking again for "Mr. Right," having forgotten my promise to the Lord.

Under conviction again, I found myself praying, "Lord, if it is your will that I go straight, please get me out of this relationship with Andy. We love each other very much, and I just cannot go through the agony of breaking another heart. All my gay life it seems that I have been breaking hearts. Please intervene; cause Andy to leave me; and I will never fail you again. I *promise*."

Again, I was making an old covenant promise to the Lord, not yet clearly understanding His new covenant in which His law was to be written in my heart, in which His will was to become my own will.

God did not answer my prayer the way I had hoped. Andy became ever more loving and doting and settled into living with me forever. It seemed that there was no way out for me. Though under severe conviction, I felt totally helpless to act upon it.

About a year earlier, when visiting and traveling to the east with my parents, I had yielded to their very persistent suggestion to stop in at a tent revival, but only for the one afternoon. I really needed to get back home to California and could not see the wisdom in this little side trip. However, at the end of the afternoon I suggested to them that we spend the night. The next day I suggested that we spend another night. I could hardly believe the beauty of the gospel as being presented at these meetings. One speaker especially was sharing Bible promises of assured victory over any and all sin through Jesus Christ.

As it turned out, this speaker lived not too far from me in southern California. One day I called him up and asked if I might come see him for some counseling. He invited me over and I went with not a little trepidation. Nervously, I shared with this pastor my experience, my conviction, and my frustration and feelings of helplessness to change my lifestyle and behavior.

He listened patiently, not batting an eye, not recoiling in horror, but with interest and compassion. Then turning in his Bible he read to me from 1 Corinthians 6:9-11,

> Know ye not that the unrighteous shall not inherit the kingdom of God? Be not deceived: neither adulterers, nor effeminate, nor abusers of themselves with mankind, Nor thieves, nor covetous, nor drunkards, nor revilers, nor extortioners, shall inherit the kingdom of God.

This was heavy! I had been fingered at least three times already in this passage, and the man was still reading,

> And such *were* some of you [his emphasis], *but* ye are washed, but ye are sanctified, but ye are justified in the name of the Lord Jesus, and by the Spirit of our God.

"You made that up!" I laughed, in a feeble attempt to make a joke. This text of Scripture really pulled the props out from under me.

"I'll read it again," he said seriously, realizing he had scored a hit and not wanting to let me skirt the issue by passing it off with a joke.

". . . And such *were* some of you," he underscored with his intonation. "You see here, Jesse, your sin is not unique; it is not new; it was prevalent throughout Bible times, and here we see it in Paul's day among the Corinthians. But notice, Paul is commending those who had gotten the victory over their besetting sins, referring to them in the past tense, stating that they were now washed, sanctified, and justified in the name of the Lord Jesus, and by the Spirit of our God."

I sat there in stunned silence, overpowered with conviction. And this man just sat there and looked at me. Finally he spoke. "Jesse, I'm not going to sit here and tell you what to do. You know what you have to do. Don't you?"

"Yes, I do," I quietly acknowledged, trembling with the realization that it was all a matter of *choice.* The ball was in my own court. All the power of heaven was standing by just waiting for me to make that *choice,* and then to sustain me in it. The Lord was not going to make it easy for me. Like the eagle chick, I was going to have to peck my way out of the mess I was in. "My grace is sufficient for you" were the words of Jesus. His strength would be added to my strength. But I had to take action.

How I dreaded going home. How could I face Andy? He knew I had been studying the Bible. He knew that I was under conviction. He sensed with foreboding that our relationship was skating on thin ice. Consequently, he had become more and more attentive and loving, hoping that somehow I would snap out of this religious phase and come back down to earth.

When I got home that night, Andy was sitting out on the deck with two place settings for dinner. As I sat down, he poured me a glass of pink Chablis. We had a few moments of cordial chit chat over the wine. Then he bluntly asked, "Are you going to leave me?"

I wasn't prepared for this. Still reeling from the shock of conviction at the pastor's house, all I wanted to do was relax and sort out my thoughts. But Andy wouldn't let me.

"You are, aren't you?" he demanded. "You really are going to give this all up. You're going to leave me and become a Jesus freak, aren't you?" By now he was trembling uncontrollably with the anguish and realization of what might be happening. With pity and my own breaking heart, I saw the little two-and-a-half-year-old boy on top of his grandma's piano in hysterics over being abandoned by his mother. And now, I was doing the same thing to him. He was now reliving the trauma of his childhood, because of me!

"I can't do this to him!" I agonized in my soul.

"You really are going to leave me, aren't you?" he asked, and broke into tears.

"Yes," I had to acknowledge. I could not lie to him, and yet I felt like my own heart was being ripped out as I confessed that I was going to follow the Lord.

Jumping up in a rage, Andy knocked over his tray and threw his glass crashing into the floor. Running into the house he screamed, "I feel like breaking things!" And break things he did. I wasn't used to violence in this man who, up to now, had only been gentle, loving, considerate, attentive and kind. He seemed to have become devil possessed. His relentless rage left me feeling totally helpless, so I let him go until he wore down.

Finally he came back to me weeping. "Please don't leave me. Please, Jesse. You're all I have."

I held him and comforted him and wept along with him. "Oh, God!" I thought to myself. "How can I leave this man and break his heart. I just can't do it. I just can not do it."

Somehow we made it through the night. I told Andy that I would try to work out an arrangement where we could stay together even though I was going to go straight. Of course that didn't work out in my favor, and we continued living as before. But, unknowingly, again, like the eagle chick in the egg, I had begun my pecking. I had taken a stand, of sorts, by admitting that I wanted to follow Jesus and go straight, that I was intending to eventually walk away from our relationship and my gay lifestyle.

As we lapsed back into our routine, it seemed as if I was as locked into our relationship as ever, not knowing how I could ever walk away. I was beginning to realize that what I had thought in the past was freedom, freedom from the law of God, was really nothing less than total bondage to Satan and sin.

Nevertheless, I continued studying my Bible and other inspirational books. One weekend Andy and I went to a gay resort in Palm Springs. Having had enough sun for one day, I found a table with a big umbrella and decided to sit in the shade and read one of my books for awhile.

Engrossed in the history of the reformation, I was unaware of an approaching patron. "Watcha readin', preacher?" he startled me back to reality.

"Oh! A book on the history of the Dark Ages and the Reformation," I responded as he nodded and passed on by.

"Preacher? Why in the world would he call me that?" I wondered. Here I was wrapped in a skimpy towel lounging by the pool at a notoriously risque gay resort, and some guy calls me preacher!

Some weeks later, hearing about an upcoming seminar on the prophecies of Daniel and Revelation, I decided to go and asked Andy to go with me. We went together for a few nights, then Andy refused to go anymore. "This stuff is pulling us apart," he lamented. But I couldn't stay away. I was fascinated by this renewed study of prophecy that I had once been so familiar with in my youth. By the time the series came to a close, my parents were visiting us again. I took them to the church that had been conducting the seminar, and wouldn't you know they would have a call that day to accept Jesus. I had many times hoped that if ever I would be able to come back to the Lord, it would be while my father was still living. It was a fervent desire of mine that he be able to see his prodigal son return home. The love of God constrained me that day, and I went forward, and my parents just happened to be there that week. They both cried, of course, but this time it was for joy.

I knew not how I could possibly make the break with Andy, but I did know the Lord was calling me again to take a stand, and I did. He would have to help me follow through.

With the stand I had now taken, it became increasingly difficult for me to remain in the same home with Andy. I began to hint more and more strongly that our days were numbered. He, in turn, upon occasion would launch into tirades of anger. One afternoon I was sitting on the toilet reading one of my books. He rushed into the bathroom, grabbed me by the ankles, yanked me off the toilet and dragged me into the bedroom before I even knew what had happened. He then pounced on my chest and started choking me. Struggling against the strength of his wrath, I broke his strangle hold and threw him off me. Yelling obscenities and profanity at me he grabbed my book and ran off to the front door.

"I'm sick of your books," he yelled! "They're outta here!" He then proceeded to throw my book into the street. Racing around the house, he found more and threw them into the street.

Christ was working upon my heart, and I endeavored to react the way He would. Leaving him to his anger, I just prayed, "Oh, Lord, have mercy on Andy. He is distraught over the inevitable loss of what he thought would be a lifetime of security and stability. His world is crumbling around him. Please, Lord, have pity and mercy upon him."

When the storm was over, once again Andy broke down and wept uncontrollably. "Jesse, I'm sorry. I just don't want to lose you. These books are coming between us. They are taking you away from me. Please don't go away," he cried. He retrieved all but one of the books. Some passerby must have taken the one I had been reading. I never saw it again.

Again, I held him and consoled him as best I could, assuring him that my leaving would not mean that I had ceased loving him. But I would soon have to go away, for I could no longer live in a way that brought grief and pain to my God.

"Why don't you accept Him, too?" I asked.

But he could never bring himself to do so.

As my business venture was failing me financially, I could see the handwriting on the wall. The time of my departure was at hand. My car had been repossessed. I couldn't come up with my share of the rent. The Lord was truly allowing me to hit bottom, I believe, to make it easier for me to go. But where Andy was concerned, it was more difficult than anything I had ever encountered in my life.

I decided to call my parents and have them come to California and move me back home where I could start all over again. They were elated with my decision and said they would come right out. Now, to tell Andy they were coming! Two days before their arrival, I gathered my wits about me and sat him down. The time had come, and he had to know ahead of time. It was only fair.

As I revealed to him my plan, he at first just wilted on the couch. He then began to fall apart. But his weeping soon turned to rage. It was as if seven demons had been released as he pounced upon me and began pummeling with what seemed to be superhuman force. His rings gashed my face. One blow went right to my eye. At this I weakened and decided to defend myself, which only added fuel to his fire of fury. He picked up a clay planter and aimed it right at my face, but something stopped him, and he put it down. I sat back down on the couch only to be attacked again. The eye of the storm had passed, and it now resumed with a vengeance. The last I remember was the blow to the back of my head, administered by our heavy lead crystal ash tray.

Somehow Andy came to his senses and collapsed in a heap weeping uncontrollably. I went to the bathroom to nurse my wounds and didn't recognize the face staring back at me in the mirror. It looked as though I had been in an auto accident. From that point on, Andy was completely harmless. He knew he had gone too far and there was no turning back for me.

Filled with remorse, he begged my forgiveness repeatedly. I forgave him, but with resolve assured him that I would be gone in two days. He moped around in total despair, and my heart ached for him. And Satan used that in his last ditch effort to hang onto me. But I was on to Satan now. I had seen what his kingdom is like. His method of operation had been clearly exposed to me as he had used every possible means to retain me in his kingdom.

He had used popularity, money, friends, lovers, pleasure, allurements, every emotion I was capable of, and now, when all that had failed, he had turned to violence and force. None of this, however, could outweigh the love of God I now realized that had been poured out upon me, even while I was an enemy. As I beheld Him, I was being changed. His love constrained me to newness of life in Christ, a life that would bring glory and honor to my Creator, a life of selflessness rather than that of self-gratification.

As I left Andy behind, I realized I had pecked my way out of the life of bondage to sin, by the grace of God. My new life was launched with a strength and zeal I had never had before. I now understood what James meant by "the law of liberty" (James 1:25). Being in harmony with God's ten commandment law is to be living a life free from the bondage of sin. For it is by the law that we know sin, and can therefore avoid falling into the bondage thereof.

I was free at last from the clutch of Satan and sin. Jesus was truly mighty to save me *from* my sin. But could I remain free? This was the all important question. I read in 2 Peter 2:19-22,

> for of whom a man is overcome, of the same is he brought in bondage. For if after they have escaped the pollutions of the world through the knowledge of the Lord and Saviour Jesus Christ, they are again entangled therein, and overcome, the latter end is worse with them than the beginning. For it had been better for them not to have known the way of righteousness, than, after they have known it, to turn from the holy commandment delivered unto them. But it is happened unto them according to the true proverb, The dog is turned to his own vomit again; and the sow that was washed to her wallowing in the mire.

Though some Christians believe that once you are saved you will remain saved unto the end, this text was a warning to me that I would ever need to be on my guard. "Be sober, be vigilant," warns Peter, "because your adversary the devil, as a roaring lion, walketh about, seeking whom he may devour" (1 Pet. 5:8).

In these passages, I have found much encouragement to continue on in my walk with the Lord, regardless of temptation from within and from without. For if to fall back into the ways of the enemy would mean the latter end to be worse than the beginning, then what other logical *choice* is there but to continue on in the way of righteousness, with Jesus walking beside me?

SECTION SIX

Home at Last

Twenty-Two

Second Chances and
Double Portions

Fleeing California with the assistance of my parents was to me like the experience of Lot being hauled out of Sodom. It was similar to that of Moses leaving Egypt and doing the next forty years in the wilderness. I, too, decided to move to the country to do my own time in the wilderness. But after three days with my folks in the country, I got really restless. I needed to see people. I needed to see cars and traffic. Was I having withdrawals from Los Angeles gridlock? I jumped into a car and drove an hour and a half to the nearest town of any size, just so I could see people, some hustle and bustle. In a moment of weakness, I even looked for a nightclub, only to find out that I was in a dry county! Though leaving my gay life behind, I had not yet left all those *little* things behind, like cigarettes, and a few other harmful substances. But the Lord soon cleansed me of them, too.

Returning to my parents' home, I settled down to my life in the wilderness. Actually it was amazing how rapidly I adapted. I couldn't get enough of homemade bread, home canned applesauce, and frozen blueberries. And the daily walks in the fresh country air were so invigorating, as was working with my father in his garden.

"Yes," I thought. "I could really get used to this country lifestyle."

Upon accepting Jesus as my personal Savior, I had immediately realized the burden of ministering for Him in some capacity. The story of Jonah bore heavily upon my mind. He had been three days in the belly of the whale after refusing his call to minister to the people of Nineveh. I must truly have been a harder nut to crack. Sixteen years it had taken for the Lord to break through to me, and I was now very mindful of the responsibility and privilege that accompanies the acceptance of Him and His plan of salvation.

Yes, I had been a long-term Jonah. Now, "what would the Lord have me to do?" was the question weighing heavily upon my mind.

I prayed that the Lord would give me a second chance to work for Him in the ministry. My education had been in that field, so I was somewhat trained, though it had been seventeen years since my graduation. The unnerving thought came to me that because of my terrible, degraded life of sin, there might not be a place for me in the Lord's work. What church would ever want the likes of me as a pastor? And yet, the call to ministry was ever echoing within my inner being.

I then went to work to try to help the Lord answer my prayer. I had read in the Bible the story of Jesus delivering the Gadarene demoniac from his demon possession. He then wanted to follow Jesus as did the twelve disciples. However, Jesus would not allow him to serve in that capacity, but rather advised him to "Go home to thy friends, and tell them how great things the Lord hath done for thee, and hath had compassion on thee" (Mark 5:19).

My desire was to be in the ministry, but through this story I could see that perhaps Jesus had another branch of service in mind for me, like that of the delivered demoniac. So, I decided to type out my testimony and send it to everyone I could think of, telling them how great things the Lord had done for me, and of His great compassion for the likes of me.

One week later, I received a telephone call from one of my high school friends that I had not seen nor heard from in all those sixteen years. Of all people I had ever known, he was probably one of the least likely in my estimation to ever make it to the kingdom of God. But here he was on the phone telling me how he had been blessed by my testimony. It had come at just the right time to help him sort out many of his own thoughts and feelings. I have kept in touch with him ever since, and he is now strong in the faith of the Lord and zealous for righteousness.

I began to see that the Lord could indeed use my testimony in some small way to His glory and honor, and my heart thrilled with the thought of the possibilities to in some way redeem the time squandered by my reckless, selfish life.

Thinking back upon my family history, I was filled with intense remorse over the role I had played in destroying my home and family. I wondered, "Could I ever be reconciled with those I had wronged? More importantly, would they ever be reconciled to God? Would God ever give me a second chance at having a family? Would I ever be able to be married again, and have children in my home, and raise those children to be God's children? Could He ever trust me with that responsibility again?"

"No, probably not," I answered myself.

Nevertheless, I prayed for that privilege if it could be to the glory of God. "What a testimony that could be to the power of God," I thought, "to rescue the likes of me from the grasp of the enemy, one who had been torn and mangled and scarred by sin, and then re-create him into His own image once again; to restore in such a man as I, His original plan for mankind!"

As I was preparing for baptism, I reflected upon all the years squandered that I could have been living and working for the Lord. "Dear Father," I prayed. "Please grant me a double portion of Thy Holy Spirit upon my baptism. You have told us of the need to be baptized of the water and the Spirit. Please grant me a double portion of Thy Spirit that I may redeem the time for you."

My baptism was so precious to me. I entered into that water with a knowledge and awareness of the significance of this ordinance. By faith in Jesus Christ I was making a public declaration of my decision to accept Jesus into my life as Lord and Master, a public confession of my union by faith to the crucified Christ. As Jesus had closed His eyes in death for all sin, so by faith in Him I closed my eyes to be lowered into the watery tomb. By faith in Him, His burial became my burial to my old life of sin. Just as God raised Christ up from the dead by His undefeatable power, so I was brought forth from the water to newness of life in Christ. I knew that I must allow that same power to now dwell in me through the Holy Spirit, to enable me in my new Christian life.

I was fully aware of the symbology of this ordinance; that I had chosen by faith to die *with* Jesus to my life of sin, to bury with Jesus the old man of sin in the watery tomb, and to be resurrected with Christ to that newness of life in which He would now work within me to will and to do of His good pleasure in all things (Phil. 2:13). He had given me the assurance of His word that once He had begun this good work in me He would perpetuate it to the end (Phil. 1:6). I need not doubt His ability to keep me from falling back into my old life style of sin and degradation. For His promise to me was that He "is able to keep [me] from falling, and to present [me] faultless before the presence of his glory with exceeding joy" (Jude 24). He *delights* in this aspect of His work and ministry in our behalf.

Paul's words to the Hebrews I personalized in this way, "Looking unto Jesus the author and finisher of my faith; who for the joy that was set before him, the joy of spending eternity with Jesse, for this joy he endured the cross, despising the shame, and is set down at the right hand of the throne of God" (Heb. 2:2).

And so it was, in the light of these exceeding and precious promises that I prayed for second chances and double portions in order to live to His glory. And the Lord delights in answering prayer.

The very night of my baptism I was approached by a delegation from out of state who had heard my testimony at least in part, and asked me if I would come and help them open a church and serve as their pastor.

I hesitated to answer, or to commit. This was all so sudden, so unexpected.

"Have you already accepted another invitation?" they asked.

"Well, no, I haven't," I replied.

"Have you not committed to the Lord to go where ever you are invited to work for Him?"

"Yes, I have."

"Then you belong to us!" they smiled with confidence.

"Well, yes, I suppose you are right. I do. And, I will come."

"My!" I thought, "The Lord surely is quick to answer my prayer!"

As I was involved at the time in an intense Bible study program and training for evangelism, I was only able to minister to the new little church, six hours away, every third weekend. But the school was gracious enough to allow me that privilege, and thus was launched my work of ministry for the Lord.

As an indication of the double portion answer to my prayers, I received a second invitation right after my baptism. I had made it known to one of the instructors at the school that, if needed, I was willing and available to take any speaking opportunities that opened up should they ever become overly committed.

A couple nights after my baptism, there was a late night knock on the door of my little camper trailer. One of the pastors had come to ask if I could speak at the next church service. From that point on I was speaking somewhere every week. The Lord was putting me to work, and I was being richly blessed. For just as the Scripture says, "It is more blessed to give than to receive." I needed and appreciated this new dimension in my new life and was truly being blessed by it.

* * * * *

When I had written out my testimony to mail out to everyone I knew, it had been a generic one, not spelling out the specifics of my life of sin. In it I had made the statement, "The details of my life of sin are not the subject of this letter. It is not my desire to give Satan and his counterfeit for happiness any unnecessary recognition nor glorification. The purpose of this letter is to give God the glory."

However, a particular need was brought to my attention where I was asked to revise the testimony naming the specific sinful lifestyle of my past. A concerned couple wanted it thus for their own son who was homosexual.

This was very difficult for me. If the testimony fell into the wrong hands, my potential ministry could be forever damaged. It was also very difficult for me to open up this way, for there was such shame and stigma attached to the homosexual, and I just didn't know whether I could personally bear up under that stigma the rest of my life as a Christian.

As I felt more and more convicted to write just such a testimony for the benefit of homosexuals and their families, I took the matter to my higher Source of wisdom. "Father," I prayed, "if my specific testimony would in any way bring reproach upon Your name, You can keep your hand over it and prevent it from being broadcast. On the other hand, it could be that such a testimony might work to Your glory and honor. So, I will trust that if ever it is sown broadcast, that You have allowed it for that reason."

So it was that I wrote it and sent it to the family in need. Within eight months, it had been broadcast. My first knowledge of this was when visiting a congregation in a city over an hour away from our church. One of our own church members was there and approached me as I pulled up in my car for an outdoor worship service in the park.

"Pastor," she addressed me, "One of the ladies here today received a phone call from her pastor last night advising her that years ago you had left your wife and five children for the gay life in California! I just thought you ought to know before you approached that pavilion over there. Is this true?"

Caught off guard, and glancing over at the growing audience in the outdoor facility, I turned back to my concerned parishioner, "Gayle," I said with a straight face, "I don't *have* five children!" It was a poor effort to diffuse the question, and, as such, gave the answer she sought.

"Pastor, I don't care how many *children* you have!" she looked me straight in the eye with a little knowing smile. "Listen, before becoming a Christian, I was a Buddhist and a Satanist. I also hung out with a lot of gays, and even made dresses for some of the drag queens. There's nothing you can say here that will surprise me. I just want you to know that what you used to be makes no difference to *me*."

Bless her heart! She seemed to understand the good news, the gospel.

Wherefore, being tipped off, I spoke to the gathered audience on the power of God, through Jesus Christ, mighty to save to the uttermost. "My Bible says, 'that *whosoever* believeth in Him should not perish but have everlasting life.' And, as the popular chorus goes, '*who-so-ever* surely meaneth *me!*'" The people were very responsive and the message was well received.

When I returned to my church for our evening service, one of the ladies met me in the parking lot and gave me a hug saying, "Pastor, we've had a church meeting in your absence; and we just want you to know that we love you anyway." With a radiant Christian smile, she walked away.

"Sister Jones! Wait a minute!" I called after her. "What do you mean, 'anyway'?"

"Oh!" she returned. "We heard all about it, had a meeting, and decided that we like having a pastor that can demonstrate as well as preach victory over sin as you are."

I was so blessed. Mind you, the church had not been ignorant of the fact that I had been saved from a life of terrible degradation. It was, however, mutually agreed that the details were not necessary. Now that they had come out, the church was confirmed in its belief in our God who is mighty to save. Why, He could even save the *homosexual* from *his* sin!

Yes, my testimony had been broadcast. I had to trust that it was within God's plan and to His glory and honor. How else could I hold up my head, or even be seen in public? More importantly, how else could I ever stand in the pulpit? Surely the Lord knew what He was doing, and I accepted that Father knows best.

A couple of months later, I was preparing a family for baptism. One evening the mother called me up to tell me that a pastor they knew had just called them. He had proceeded to inform them of my preconversion lifestyle, to the best of his limited knowledge, obviously based itself upon false witness, to which the little mother replied, "Yes, but, Pastor, don't you believe in victory over sin?"

His response was typical of many Christians who may have "a form of godliness, but denying the *power* thereof" (2 Tim. 3:5).

"Yes, of course," he replied. "But *that* kind can never change! And, furthermore, I would advise you to keep your children away from this man!"

The insinuation, of course, was that I had also been, and perhaps remained, a pedophile, a child molester. Ouch! The story being broadcast was taking on unexpected new dimensions!

A friend had earlier attempted to set at ease my paranoia saying, "Jesse, don't worry about what enemies might say. If they don't have something on you, they would just make up something."

"Make up something?" I rejoined. "What's to make up? How could they make up anything worse than what's true about me?"

Well, here it was! I was terribly shaken in shocked disbelief. Children! It never crossed my mind that I would be accused of that! You see, even a homosexual can find someone else's sin to be more repulsive than his own, to be socially unacceptable.

This unfortunate pastor, like so many others, mistakenly believed that homosexuality and pedophilia are one and the same thing, or at best, inseparably linked. However, their only relation to each other is that both are a perversion of what sexuality was designed to be by our loving Creator, as is any sexual behavior outside the marriage institution. Statistics show that most pedophilia is heterosexual, not homosexual.

Praise the Lord for this family, however, who did believe in victory over sin through the blood of the Lamb and the word of my testimony (Rev. 12:11). Several weeks later, I immersed them, along with nine other believers, in the watery grave of baptism as they decided to die with Jesus by faith; die to sin and self, to bury the old man of sin, and to be resurrected into newness of life by faith in Jesus Christ Who gave His own life that "*whosoever* believeth in Him should not perish, but have everlasting life" (John 3:16).

Before I could come up out of the water, my own father stepped down into the water fully dressed, tears of joy trickling down his cheeks in heart appreciation for what the Lord had wrought in his own life and in that of his son. As I baptized Dad, there was hardly a dry eye in the on looking crowd. They all knew the story.

"I want what you have, Jesse," Dad said. "I want the same power of the Holy Spirit to work in my life that I now see working in yours."

"How could I ever have wasted all those years in the world?" I thought as we embraced in the water. "My life all along could have been one of fulfillment such as this in the ministry of the good news of the incomprehensible gift of the Father in the offering of His only begotten Son for the redemption of the lost human race! It just couldn't get any better than this?"

*   *   *   *   *

Being single, a new pastor, and in the ministry soon revealed to me an unexpected danger. Pastors, of course, are supposed to be above reproach and suspicion at all times and in every way. It became difficult for me to function effectively in ministry without a wife. My friendliness was eventually mistaken for interest in some cases. And my inexperience proved to be a detriment.

In the gay world I had felt at liberty to throw caution to the wind in my everyday interaction with women, because they were no temptation to me whatsoever. My motives were never to seduce, or to score with them, but rather to just enjoy their friendship and to socialize with them. And those who really knew me appreciated being able to likewise throw caution to the wind without any danger of being perceived as inviting pursuit.

In my new life, this attitude toward women had mistakenly not yet been corrected. I was resigned to the likelihood of living the celibate life of Paul the apostle, or Jesus Christ, if necessary. After all, many people, because of illness, disabili-

ties, unique personalities, responsibilities, divorce, being wid-
owed, and countless other circumstances, live their lives without the pleasures and privileges of matrimony, even though
they would dearly love to be married if they could.

Of course, there are even some who *choose* to never have
those pleasures and privileges God has given to the institution
of marriage alone. But these such Christians are not necessarily
sacrificing anything in this respect; they are perfectly content to
live lives of celibacy. To them abstinence may not be a matter
of self-denial at all, but rather a lifestyle of freedom and inde-
pendence.

This second scenario was not the one to which I could
relate. But, rather, the first one; the one which required a life
of self-denial. And, I decided, so be it. I am not worthy of a
second chance in this area anyway, I reasoned. And the Lord
only knows if I, as a husband, could even fulfill the expectations of a woman and a wife.

But my pastoral effectiveness began to suffer the longer I
remained single. There were those who doubted my victory,
not knowing where I was and what I was doing at all times.
One member of our church came to me on more than one
occasion with the observation that he never knew anyone con-
verted from homosexuality who lasted more than two years!
Well, that was certainly not a word of encouragement on his
part! I eventually wrote him a letter asking that instead of
waiting on the sidelines for me to fall in accordance with his
prediction, why not lift me up in prayer that I would *not* fall
back into sin.

Then there were those who thought I should be married,
and even had suggestions for me. Still others advised that I
should never remarry, that I had no Biblical grounds to ever do
so again. I wished people would just leave me alone on this
subject. I was not prepared to be involved with women romantically. In fact, I was still very sensitive to the grief and pain I
had so recently wrought upon one who loved me, and was
quite gun shy about any more relationships.

However, the Lord had His own solution and plan in
mind. In coming back to Him one year earlier, I had looked up

and renewed my acquaintance with Rachel and her husband; Rachel being the little girl from high school who had been a friend of my sisters' and remained so these thirty years. Two weeks after meeting her and her husband again, he walked out on her, divorced her, and married someone else. Being brotherly, I had kept in touch with her throughout the entire ordeal, consoling her, praying with her, encouraging her. It was months after he had remarried that Rachel finally told me; and all this time I had been praying that her husband would return to her.

"She's available!" I blurted out one day in the presence of two other pastors I was traveling with. It had been slow in dawning upon me, but suddenly I realized that Rachel had been set free by an unbelieving husband who had departed (1 Cor. 7).

"What?" they reacted. "Who's available? What are you talking about?"

"Rachel!" I said. "She's available. All this time I've been praying for her failed marriage. And her husband has already remarried! Months ago!"

"Who's Rachel?" they asked.

Calming down, I then told them the whole story, to their great interest.

Up until then, I had not known whether pursuing a lady for marriage was something I could even do. Having been so many years emotionally involved with men, was I even capable of loving and cherishing a woman? If not, then why my sudden awareness of Rachel's availability and the excitement beating in my heart?

I initiated a courtship with her and we fell mutually in love. She told me that she had been in love with me for thirty years, beginning in high school when I was in love with her roommate Tina. I had been romantically interested in various close friends of hers when she was the one I should have paid attention to.

But the Lord had saved the best till last. Rachel became the love of my life, eclipsing the loves and relationships of the past.

"I don't know what your brother is up to," she had told my sister who later shared the encouragement with me, "but I sure wish he'd hurry up!"

So, I did. After all, we had known each other for thirty years. Being friends with my sisters, she knew my sordid life history and was thrilled with my new found faith. In fact, her faith had to be as strong as mine, if not stronger, in order to take on the commitment to someone with my history. After much prayer about it, we both believed that God was working in behalf of both of us. It was a somewhat brief courtship and engagement, and then we were married.

Rachel had a ten year old child, and I thought, "Surely the Lord has answered my prayers in a marvelous way. He has given me a second chance in the ministry. Now he has given me a second chance with a family. Once again, I have it all; the best of all worlds this side of heaven."

Two years later we discovered that in our "old age" we were expecting a child of our own. Our wedding had been based upon the theme of Isaac and Rebecca. Now the joke was that we were more like Abraham and Sarah. Actually, we were only in our forties. During a prenatal visit one day, the midwife asked, "Are there any twins in your family?"

"Twins! Jesse-eee! No, there are no twins; not that we are aware of!" Rachel answered with trepidation.

"Twins," laughed her visiting mother popping into the room after overhearing the question. "Why, yes, of course! Let's see there was your uncle and aunt on this side of the family . . . and then there were your two cousins on that side; and, let me see . . ."

"Mom! Why haven't I ever heard about this before?" Rachel whimpered.

My visiting mother then came into the room, face beaming gleefully, having also been listening from outside. "My aunt lost a twin brother at birth. And, Jesse, your grandpa had twin sisters!"

"Jesse!" Rachel pleaded in mocked desperation. "It's time for you to stop praying for those second chances and double portions, you hear?"

Then we all broke out in hearty laughter. Twins! How exciting!

As it turned out, however, four months later Rachel gave birth to one, our beautiful little son. After naming him, we discovered the meaning of his name to be "the Lord has remembered." And surely He had. The double portion came nineteen months later with our precious little girl. Another nineteen months and another child was due! However, due to illness, the pregnancy failed to go full term. It was twins, another little boy and girl. These two we look forward to raising in heaven where they will never know sin and sorrow, pain, nor death.

More than I could ever have expected or imagined, the Lord had truly answered my prayer for "second chances and double portions." Surely He was Himself smiling with pleasure and delight for the wonders He had wrought.

The whole idea behind God's plan of salvation is that of second chances. It is a work of reconciliation; turning the hearts of the created back to their loving Creator; turning the hearts of the fathers to the children, and the children to their fathers. It is an unmerited, but marvelous work of reclamation, recreation, and restoration back to that which our Father knows is best for us His children.

As my recurring nightmare had been a foretaste of being forever lost, the reconciliation God has wrought within my family has become a foretaste of heaven. The mutual forgiveness, love, and respect that now exists between the members of our family, all testify to the power of God to save His people from their sins. True, He is not finished with any of us yet. But it can be seen that God is working within us to will and to do of His good pleasure, to ultimately bring about our total reconciliation with Himself.

Today, by the divine influence working upon his heart and being reflected in his life, by grace, my father is a humble, sweet and dear man, greatly beloved by all his children and by everyone who knows him. He loves and is very proud of all his children. It almost never fails, that whenever I am standing in the pulpit or performing special music, I will notice Dad in the audience struggling to hold back the tears of joy and gratitude, striving to control his emotions. His prodigal son has come home.

Scripture tells us that all heaven rejoices over one sinner that repents. God, in His unselfish love for us His children, wants us to share in His joy. Sometimes that means that we must share in His sorrow as well. For only then can we truly appreciate His marvelous gift of redemption and salvation.

I truly believe there is a corollary between sorrow and joy; that the deeper the suffering of sorrow and pain, the greater the heights of joy one is prepared to experience. Therefore, those who have suffered the greatest depths of sorrow may hold onto the hope of future exaltation in joy and happiness. ". . . But to whom little is forgiven, the same loveth little" (Luke 7:47). The inference is that to whom much is forgiven, the same loveth much. The greater the sorrow, the greater the capacity for joy.

One of the strongest evidences I have seen of the reconciliation power of God was on a recent trip to visit Stephanie and Donnie out west. The meeting place was at the home of their mother, Leanne. What could have been an awkward evening was instead filled with delightful interaction between all the members of "the family." After all the good-byes were said, everyone loaded up into the car to leave. But, where was Mommy? We waited for quite some time, and I then went in to help Rachel find her way out of Leanne's home. Approaching the door, I saw them embracing one another and sharing words of comfort and encouragement.

My Rachel and Leanne were friends! Only in the kingdom of heaven could this be! What a foretaste of what is yet to come! God is certainly good.

Twenty-Three

You, Too, Can Be Made Whole!

"I've never known anyone coming from a homosexual lifestyle who has ever been able to remain straight for more than two years!"

"Sure I believe in victory over sin. But *that* kind can never change!"

"You'd better keep your children away from him!"

"I've been a preacher for forty years, and I've never met a perfect person yet!"

If you are a sin sick soul seeking deliverance from bondage in *this* life, how do remarks such as these affect you? Do they give you hope, or leave you despondent and in despair?

Statements such as these coming from the mouths of some Christians reveal their focus to be upon the ability and works of man, the sinner, the helpless victim, rather than upon the omnipotent ability and works of the Savior. They unwittingly portray God as impotent, rather than omnipotent. He it is who has promised to save you, dear reader, from sin. He it is who has promised to cleanse you, to work within you, to perform that good work He has begun in you until the day of Jesus Christ, to keep you from falling and to present you faultless. He it is that paid the infinite price for your redemption. He has a vested interest in you and will finish what He has started, if you will only stop resisting Him. He is the Alpha and the Omega, the first and the last, the beginning and the end. He is not a quitter!

Without this understanding, what hope does the Christian have to offer any sin sick soul who wants deliverance *in this life* from the bondage of sin? Without this understanding, the best the Christian can portray to the world is a *form* of godliness, denying the *power* thereof. The call for repentance can be heard from every pulpit in the land, but when a homosexual repents, too many Christians reveal their lack of faith in the God of love Who is mighty to save *to the uttermost,* and express doubt in the ability of the victim to be saved by the Savior.

As I, by God's grace, was leaving behind my homosexual life, a gay friend of mine who himself had been a pastor for several years made the following statement. "Jesse, I'm going to be keeping my eye on you. If you last for two years in the straight world, then I'll believe that just maybe I would be able to do the same."

I pray to God that this dear friend of the past will somehow find this book in his hands, for at the time of publication of this book, it will have been *nine* years of victorious living for me.

Friend, you, too, can be made whole!

May the following suggestions help you find restoration and victory at last, even as they have been so sustaining for me.

1) *Know, and believe:* first of all *that "God is love"* (1 John 4:8). Know and believe that whoever you are, whatever you are, God loves you unconditionally, just as you are. For God the Father so loved you, the homosexual, that He gave His only begotten son, that *whosoever* believeth in Him (whosoever means even the homosexual), should not perish, but have everlasting life (John 3:16). He loved the world, as it was, and poured out His love upon the world in the gift of His son, demonstrating and revealing that incomprehensible love, while the world was still in rebellion. His love has been manifested toward you, the sinner, the homosexual, in that while you are yet at odds with Him and His will for you; yes, even while you see Him as the enemy, blaming Him for everything wrong in your life; even while in this attitude of enmity toward Him, He poured out His love for you in the gift of His Son.

"For when we were yet without strength, in due time Christ died for the ungodly. [That includes you!] But God commendeth his love toward us, in that, while we were yet sinners, Christ died for us . . . when we were enemies, we were reconciled to God by the death of his Son" (Rom. 5:6, 8, 10).

God the Father paid the redemptive price for you, which just happens to be the infinite cost of His own Son, knowing who and what you are before you were ever born. As with Jeremiah, He can say of you, "Before I formed thee in the belly, I knew thee" (Jer. 1:5).

"Not only that, knowing that you would become homosexual, I paid the redemptive price for you, allowed you to be born, loving you anyway and wanting to spend eternity with you. Therefore, I have preserved you in life with a stay of execution provided by My only begotten Son, even though you have been totally out of sync with my plan for you up to this point. But, if you will slow down and look at Me, comprehend how much I love you, and allow Me the opportunity, I can and will save you personally from your lifestyle of sin. I can heal you, recreate you, wash you and make you clean. It is your choice. May I have you for my very own?"

God is love, and He loves you with an immeasurable love, regardless of whether you love Him back or not. In the end, the lake of fire of Revelation 20:10,13 will be the final resting place for billions of people whom God loves unconditionally. But they have rejected that love, refusing to respond by allowing Him to prepare them with a fitness to dwell in His presence for all eternity. Sin is consumed in His presence. If it is enthroned in the heart, the soul will be consumed with the sin.

2) Now, step up to the mirror and *face yourself.* Do not be afraid to take an honest look at who and what you really are. Eternal reality is the real issue to consider. If you are truly okay, then it doesn't hurt to examine yourself closely. Truth can bear scrutiny. So scrutinize your condition and your position.

Jesus invites you with great love, compassion, and sincere personal interest in you, *whosoever* you may be: "Come now, and *let us reason together*." He pleads with you, "Though your sins be as scarlet, don't be afraid to come to me; they shall be as white as snow, I promise; though they be red like crimson, don't refuse me; they shall be as wool, I promise. If you be willing and obedient, you shall eat the good of the land, I promise: But *only* if you refuse and rebel in determined stubbornness and self-deception, shall you be devoured" (Isa. 1:18, 19; paraphrased and personalized).

3) *Acknowledge:* who and what you really are. Face up to it; you are a sinner. "For all have sinned and come short of the glory of God" (Rom. 3:23). Don't deny it, for you will only be deceiving yourself to your own eternal ruin.

> Only acknowledge thine iniquity, that thou hast transgressed against the Lord thy God. Turn, O backsliding children, saith the Lord; for I am married unto you. You have perverted your way and forgotten the Lord your God. Return, ye backsliding children. Come back to me, and I will heal your backslidings. (Jer. 3:13, 14, 21, 22; paraphrased)

If you will but confess your sin, God is faithful and just to not only forgive you of your sin, but to also cleanse you from *all* unrighteousness; to change you; to recreate you into His image, into His character (1 John 1:9).

4) *Realize:* The wages of your sin is no greater nor less than the wages of the sins of others who may have a particular disdain for your particular besetting sin. For the wages of any sin is death. Yes, the Bible does call homosexuality abomination. The Bible seems to call all sin abomination. Notice: "If a man also lie with mankind, as he lieth with a woman, both of them have committed an abomination" (Lev. 20:13; 18:22).

Other abominations include idolatry (Deut. 13:14); an impure sacrifice (Deut. 17:1); occultic practices (Deut. 18:10-12); wearing that which pertaineth to the opposite sex (Deut. 22:5); certain re-marriages to former spouses (Deut. 24:4); dishonesty (Deut. 25:13-16); perverse behavior (Deut. 3:32); a proud look, a lying tongue, murder, wicked imaginations, mischief, false witness that speaks lies, and he that sows discord among brethren (Prov. 6:16-19); justifying evil and condemning the just (Prov. 17:15); adultery (Ezek. 22:11).

It should especially be noticed in this line up of abominations that adultery of *any kind* is included. The heterosexual sinner need not look down his nose with condescension upon the homosexual sinner, for *any* sexual behavior outside the marriage institution as designed and created by God is sin and an abomination. In short, we all need a Savior, from sin, from abomination of one kind or another.

5) *Understand:* If you are homosexual, *it matters not how you became so.* Being *born* homosexual, *choosing* to be so, or being environmentally *conditioned* to be so is not the issue that should really be of concern. Rather, how do we arouse you, the homosexual, to your need, if there is one; and how do we answer to that *need,* regardless of how and why you happen to be what you are? Do we just accept homosexuality in ourselves or in others as an acceptable alternative lifestyle, or do we see a need for redirection, and a means to accomplish that end? Is the issue of homosexuality a salvation issue, or is it a non-issue? Is it an eternal reality issue? Did Jesus come to save the homosexual *in* his homosexuality, or *from* his homosexuality? (Matt. 1:21).

Perhaps a simple little allegory can illustrate this point:

A person floundering helplessly in the stormy sea is happened upon by a lifeboat. As it draws up alongside the helpless victim, before throwing out the life line, the life guard calls out to him over the din of the screaming wind and billowing waves the qualifying questions, "How did you get yourself into this predicament anyway? Did you fall off your boat, or did you jump in? Did someone playfully push you into the sea, or did someone maliciously throw you in? Is it my fault that you are drowning in this sea? Something I have done? Are you in this plight against your will, through no fault of your own, or did you *choose* to swim out here of your own volition?"

The spitting, sputtering victim weakly calls back, "No! I did not *choose* to be this way!"

Having now qualified the drowning victim, the all important questions being answered, the lifeguard skillfully throws out the lifeline, only to see the victim refuse to grab hold.

"Take hold!" shouts the lifeguard.

"What's the use?" calls back the drowning victim. "I didn't *choose* to be in this quandary!"

And so the allegory ends in tragedy.

In just such a light, many homosexuals and heterosexuals alike view their own state in life. More grievous than this, so do many people picture Jesus the Lifeguard and His plan of salvation, as qualifying the victim first, as if God cannot, or chooses not, to save to the uttermost!

The *good news,* however, is that unlike the allegory above, Jesus cares not how you became the homosexual or sinner that you may be! Whether you are in denial, latent, in the closet, openly gay, married, militant, or even a flaming queen, the fact still remains: if you are a homosexual, you are a sinner. However, Jesus is mighty to save *you*. He has come as the Lifeguard, asking no questions, except "Will you take my hand?"

"Come unto me," he says, "and I will give you rest" (Matt. 11:28).

God's re-creative plan of salvation and redemption is as much for the homosexual, sin sick and desperate for deliverance, as it is for any other element of society, all of whom were born with inherited tendencies to sin of one kind or another that were later cultivated.

Every baby ever born was born with a *self-centered nature* that must be overcome if he is to become fit for the kingdom of heaven and God. Every person on earth living in sin of any kind is only doing that which comes natural from a heart centered in self-gratification: the murderer, the liar, the thief, the drug addict, the whoremonger, the street walker, the alcoholic, the smoker, the overeater, the cheating spouse, the promiscuous teenager, the idolater seeking to avenge an angry god or working for reward, the Christian likewise obeying God in fear of punishment or hope of reward; all are allowing self to be their rule of faith and practice.

Homosexuality is but one of many fruits, or manifestations, of the innocuous root of self. Self-gratification is paramount in this sexual orientation. Pride is also very rooted in the heart of the homosexual; as is covetousness, wanting that which God has forbidden us to have. Like the forbidden fruit in the garden of Eden, homosexual behavior is forbidden by the explicit Word of God.

Three sins especially offensive to God are pride, selfishness, and covetousness (Isa. 14:12-15; 28:17; 2 Pet. 2:9, 10; Psa. 10:3). Why? They are not so easily detected, being as they are the hidden roots of all other sins. They are the sins of the heart that manifest themselves, perhaps, many years later in outward fruit. They are the sins that festered in the heart of Lucifer in heaven that worked so successfully to deceive his own self and one third of all the angels of heaven who stood in the very presence of God Almighty. They are the sins that eventually made a devil out of Lucifer and broke the heart of God. Is it any wonder then that these sins are so offensive to Him?

Recognizing your need will be a major accomplishment, a major stepping stone, on your road to restoration.

6) *Accept the fact: It's all about choices.* God created everyone of us with the power of choice. This is the only barrier He cannot and will not cross, the only obstacle He cannot surmount in your behalf. He must have your permission to wash you, to make you clean, to create within you a clean heart, and to renew a right spirit within you; to re-create you. Ask and you shall receive!

Never forget that you are in good Company. Jesus Himself had to die to self daily and choose to follow His Father's will. The warfare against self is the greatest battle ever fought, and Jesus had to fight it, too.

"If any man will come after me, let him deny himself, and take up his cross daily, and follow me" (Luke 9:23). If He asks you to follow Him in daily self-denial, then He also had to daily practice denial of self.

"I can of mine own self do nothing." He says, "I seek not mine own will, but the will of the Father which hath sent me" (John 5:30).

"O my Father, if it be possible, let this cup pass from me: nevertheless not as I will, but as thou wilt" (Matthew 26:39). "Not as I want," He said, "but as You want." And this in agony of soul struggling against His own will in Gethsemane.

Jesus' daily victory was based upon His daily choices, sustained by the power afforded Him from God, even as the same is promised to you and me through the working of the Holy Spirit in the life.

7) *Walk with God:* It is vital that you develop and maintain a relationship with God through communion with Him in prayer and Bible study. He is the power Source for your victorious life. As your Creator, He has selfless love for you and the power to re-create you into His own image. Daily devotion time, plugging in, making that connection with Him, is of utmost importance, for in no other way can you really get to know and appreciate Him and tap into His strength.

This was the secret of success for Daniel, of whom there is no recorded sin in the Bible, though we know that "all [including Daniel] have sinned, and come short of the glory of God" (Rom. 3:23). Evidently, Daniel was an overcomer, living the victorious life as one who had been made whole. What was his practice in this respect? "Now when Daniel knew that the writing was signed, he went into his house; and his windows being open in his chamber toward Jerusalem, he kneeled upon his knees three times a day, and prayed, and gave thanks before his God, as he did aforetime" (Dan. 6:10).

Apparently, Daniel spent as much time and frequency in communing with God, his power Source, feeding himself spiritually, as he spent in feeding himself physically.

Enoch is another example of one who maintained victory through a close connection with his power Source. "And Enoch walked with God: and he was not; for God took him" (Gen. 5:24).

You, too, can have what Enoch had. You, too, can have Christ as your constant companion. Enoch walked with God, and when assaulted by the enemy with temptation, he could talk with Him about it. He made God his confidant and counselor, maintaining a close relationship with Him.

While trusting in your heavenly Father for the help you may need, He will not leave you. God has a heaven full of blessings that He wants to bestow upon you, if you are earnestly seeking for that help which only He can give. It was in looking by faith to Jesus, in asking Him in prayer, in believing that every word spoken by God would be verified, that Enoch walked with God. He kept close by the side of God, obeying His every word. Christ was his companion, and He longs to be yours.

8) *Protect your environment:* Guard well the avenues to your soul. Do not place yourself in the path of temptation. Be careful what you watch, what you read, what you behold, what you hear. Give Satan no advantage over you. "Whatsoever things are true . . . honest . . . just, whatsoever things are pure . . . lovely . . . of good report; if there be any virtue, and if there be any praise, think on these things" (Phil. 4:8).

And when Satan plants those impure thoughts and desires into your heart, (and he will), Paul bids you take every thought captive, "bringing into captivity every thought to the obedience of Christ" (2 Cor. 10:5). Use your power of choice to "change the subject." God will help you do this, if you choose.

"Submit [yourself] therefore to God. Resist the devil, and he will flee from you" (James 4:7).

9) *Immerse yourself: into the context of Scripture.* Personalize it as in the following example using Isaiah 53:3-7, 11, 12:

> As I in my homosexuality was despised and rejected by society, even so, and because of me, Jesus was despised and rejected of men; As I sorrowed and grieved over losing my children because of my bondage to sin, even so Jesus was a man of sorrows, and acquainted with my personal grief: and, not appreciating his empathy and sympathy, I hid as it were my face from him; I turned my back to him and walked away, blaming Him for every consequence of my own bad choices. But, and nonetheless, as a willing substitute for me, he was really the one despised, and I never realized it.
>
> Surely he has borne my griefs, and carried my sorrows: yet I did not appreciate his being stricken, smitten of

God, and afflicted for the sake of my falling into the sin of homosexuality.

But he was wounded for my transgressions of the seventh commandment of His law, he was bruised for the sake of my lifestyle of sin: the somewhat peace of mind I experienced by giving up the battle resulted in reproach upon him; and, looking to the cross, realizing the infinite selfless love for me that put him there, beholding his bruised and bleeding body in my place, all this has brought healing to me, reconciliation toward him. For, how could anyone not respond to that incomprehensible totally selfless love manifested toward me even while I have maintained my rebellion against him?

All of us, not just the homosexual, but all of us like sheep have gone astray in one way or another; we have turned every one to his own way. We are all naturally self-centered; and the Lord has laid on Jesus the iniquities of every one of us.

He was oppressed as some of us are, and for our sakes; and he was afflicted as some of us are, and for our sakes; yet he opened not his mouth in complaint, but endured willingly anticipating the joy of seeing me respond and return to him in love and appreciation. He is brought as an innocent, obedient, compliant lamb to the slaughter, and as a sheep before her shearers is dumb, so he opened not his mouth in self-defense, or seeking self-preservation.

He shall see the results someday of the travail, the anguish, the heartache, the suffering and misery of his soul, and shall be satisfied, as I finally respond with a heart appreciation that will cause me to live no longer for self-exaltation, self-ambition, and self-gratification. No! But to honor him, to exalt him, to gratify his selfless will for the good of his creation. Through a knowledge and understanding of what he has done for all mankind, including homosexuals, many shall be brought back into a right relationship with their Creator; that means many homosexuals shall also be brought back into a right relationship with their Creator; for he shall bear their iniquities, the wages of which is the second, or eternal, death.

He was numbered with the transgressors, with the likes of you and me, homosexual sinners and heterosexual sinners, yet he did not participate in our sinful behavior. He did, however, bare the sin of every one of us, and made intercession, arbitration, intervention for us the disobedient ones.

Another one:

Therefore if any man be in Christ. . . . "Any man" must include me the homosexual! Then I, too, am a new creature: old things are passed away; behold, all things are become new. And now all things are of God, now according to his will and pleasure, not my own; God, who hath reconciled us to himself by Jesus Christ, and hath given to us the ministry of reconciliation. (2 Cor. 5:18; paraphrased and personalized)

10) *Act: upon His word.* There is power in the word of God. "And God said, Let there be light: and there was light" (Gen. 1:3).

"For he spake, and it was done; he commanded, and it stood fast" (Psa. 33:9).

"The just shall live by faith" (Heb. 10:38), we are told. Faith in what? Faith in the Word, Jesus Christ. When Jesus spoke to Mary, saying "Neither do I condemn thee: go, and sin no more" (John 8:11), she was enabled by faith in His word.

There hath no temptation taken you but such as is common to man: but God is faithful, who will not suffer you to be tempted above that ye are able; but will with the temptation also make a way to escape that ye may be able to bear it. (1 Cor. 10:13)

"Now unto him that is able to do exceeding abundantly above all that we ask or think, according to the power that worketh in us" (Eph. 3:20).

"I can do all things through Christ which strengtheneth me" (Phil. 4:13).

"Greater is he that is in you, than he that is in the world" (1 John 4:4).

All God's biddings, dear reader, are enablings. So, take these and other promises of the Word and act upon them.

11) *Be grateful:* Accept with gratitude that which God *has* offered you. In the Garden of Eden, God created a helpmate for Adam: a woman. In His infinite wisdom and love for the well-being of man, He gave him the gift of a woman to be by his side. There was no alternative. So, did God make a mistake? Did He not know what He was doing? Did He somehow not understand the needs of the man He Himself had just created?

I have children. While on one of my recent engagements overseas I went to great lengths to find what I thought would be a very special surprise for them. I searched in each country I visited for what I had in mind. Finally, I found them. Arriving home at the airport, I had them sticking out the top of my backpack.

"What's that?" they both asked excitedly.

"I have a surprise for you," I said.

"What is it?" they jumped up and down in excitement.

I took down my back pack and gave them each a doll. Little Heidi I gave to my little girl, and little Peter I gave to my little boy. I just knew they would both love these little treasures, because they both played house and "mommy and daddy" with little dolls all the time.

"I don't want it!" whispered my little boy.

"Why not?" I asked in surprise. "You are always wanting to play with your sister's little dolls, so I brought you one of your very own!"

"I don't like it" he answered. "I like hers."

"Well, I'm sorry," I said with great disappointment. "Heidi is for your sister."

My special gift purchased at such "great price" and effort was spurned by my little boy. I had to put it away in the attic, hoping that someday he would appreciate it and want it. (I love him still; he is very dear and precious to me.)

Likewise, God went to great lengths to provide for man the wonderful gift of woman. Some of us have turned up our noses at this gift, and, instead, burn in our lust for one another. Does God stop loving us? No! Of course not. Does he give us the gift that he has created for someone else, that he has provided for the woman? No! It is with great disappointment that he sees man covet for himself what was meant by the Creator to be for the woman.

It is not a sin to do without the gift. But it is wrong for us men to covet what He has forbidden, that which was meant for the woman. It is equally wrong for the woman to lust and covet after another woman whom God has created for man.

"In everything give thanks: for this is the will of God in Christ Jesus concerning you" (1 Thess. 5:18).

"Rejoice in the Lord alway" (Phil. 4:4).

Be grateful for what God has provided for your best interest. Father truly knows best!

12) *The Secret to overcoming* the sin of homosexuality, or any other besetting sin, is in helping someone else to overcome his sin. This premise is based upon the heavenly principle for happiness: self-*less*-ness. True happiness comes in helping someone else be happy: Jesus first, others second, yourself last creates the acronym for JOY.

Joseph, far from home in the land of his captivity, never forgot this principle. "How can I do this great wickedness and sin against God?" he cried as he fled from the temptation of Potiphar's wife. His concern was not fear of punishment, nor was it hope of reward. No, for his faithfulness in obedience resulted in disgrace and confinement to the dungeon. Joseph's concern was a total self-*less* interest in the will and pleasure and honor of his God; regardless of consequences. He also loved and honored his master Potiphar, putting his interests above his own.

All the heavenly host is focused upon the happiness and well-being of others—yours, for example! All creation, except for sinful man, lives for the benefit of the rest of creation.

The apostle John gave us the concise formula for victory as follows: "And they overcame him [the accuser of our brethren] by the blood of the Lamb, and by the word of their testimony" (Rev. 12:11).

From the day of my deliverance and victory, I have lived to share the story of "the blood of the Lamb," the incomprehensible demonstration of the love of God for the likes of me that would constrain Him to give His only begotten Son that I, even I the homosexual, might have eternal life with Him! What a price! What love He has for me!

By the word of my testimony to others, this love and power of God is kept ever fresh in my own heart and mind. By beholding Him, I am daily changed and sustained in victory. In the face of such beautiful love, I can, like Joseph, respond to the tempter, "How can I do this great wickedness and sin against my God?"

Jesus told the cleansed Gadarene demoniac, "Go home to thy friends, and tell them how great things the Lord hath done for thee, and hath had compassion on thee" (Mark 5:19). He has enjoined me to do the same, and through this book I have.

And I pass along to you, dear reader, this same commission. Now, why don't you also "Go home to thy friends, and tell them how great things the Lord hath done for thee, and hath had compassion on thee?"

When you hear someone say about you, or about someone else, "*That* kind can never change!" Do not believe it, nor accept it. For *you, too, can be made whole!*

Benediction:

> Now the God of peace, that brought again from the dead our Lord Jesus, that great shepherd of the sheep, through the blood of the everlasting covenant, Make *you* perfect in *every* good work to do *his* will, working in *you* that which is well-pleasing in *his* sight, through Jesus Christ; to whom be glory for ever and ever. Amen. (Heb. 13:20, 21; emphasis added)

We welcome comments from our readers. Feel free to write to us at the following address:

Editorial Department
Huntington House Publishers
P.O. Box 53788
Lafayette, LA 70505

or visit our website at:

www.huntingtonhousebooks.com

===

More Good Books from Huntington House Publishers & Prescott Press

The Deadly Deception
Freemasonry Exposed..
By One of It's Top Leaders
by Jim Shaw and Tom McKenny

This is the story of one man's climb to the top, the top of the "Masonic mountain." A climb that uncovered many "secrets" enveloping the popular fraternal order of Freemasonry. Shaw brings to life the truth about Freemasonry, both good and bad, and for the first ever, reveals the secretive Thirty-Third Degree initiation

ISBN 0-910311-54-4

The Hidden Dangers of the Rainbow
by Constance Cumbey

This nationwide best-seller paved the way for all other books on the subject of the New Age movement. Constance Cumbey's book reflects years of in-depth and extensive research. She clearly demonstrates the movement's supreme purpose: to subvert our Judeo-Christian foundation and create a one-world order through a complex network of occult organizations. Cumbey details how these various organizations are linked together by common mystical experiences. The author discloses who and where the leaders of this movement are and discusses their secret agenda to destroy our way of life.

ISBN 0-910311-03-X

A Divine Appointment in Washington DC
by James F. Linzey

A spiritual tool on praying in the Spirit and a scholarly tool for the classroom, A Divine Appointment in Washington DC includes testimonials, study guide, index, and a recommended reading list. The author has appeared on television networks such as the Oasis Television Network and Trinity Broadcasting Network.

ISBN 1-56384-169-X

E–vangelism
Sharing the Gospel in Cyberspace
by Andrew Careaga

Cyberspace has become a repository for immense spiritual yearning. The Internet is reshaping the way we work, interact, learn, communicate, and even pray. Provided are ideas for building a website and helpful guides for Christians to find their way around the maze of chat rooms, discussion groups, and bulletin boards found on the Internet.

ISBN 1-56384-160-6

Good-bye America?
by Jonathan West

Congress is a mess, the White House is a disgrace, lawyers are bleeding us to death, the government bureaucracy is becoming a massive dictatorship, and the cost of it all is taxing us to our limits and beyond. Can anything reasonable be done? Is there an intelligent answer? You bet there is!

ISBN 0-933451-46-6

En Route to Global Occupation
A High Ranking Government Liaison Exposes the Secret Agenda for World Unification
by Gary H. Kah

Kah warns that national sovereignty will soon be a thing of the past. Political forces around the world are now cooperating in unprecedented fashion to achieve their goal of uniting the people of this planet under a New World Order.

ISBN 0-910311-97-8

The 3 Loves of Charlie Delaney
by Joey W. Kiser

A delightful story of first love, innocence, heartbreak, and redemption. Kiser uses his pen to charm and enchant but most of all...to remind.

ISBN 0-933451-45-8

How to Avoid High Tech Stress
by Robert J. du Puis, M.D.

Technology has created "Instruments of Urgency." such as E-mail, fax machines, cellular phones and pagers, which allow instant communication and transfer of information. It also allows instant accessibility unknown in the past. *How to Avoid High Tech Stress* examines how this instant accessibility has caused increasing levels of stress—instead of freeing us from drudgery.

ISBN 1-56384-159-2

Revelation and the Rapture Unveiled!
by Frank Hart

Revelation and the Rapture Unveiled! is an inductive Bible study of the key prophetic pattern for the fulfillment of events that surround the Second Coming of Jesus Christ and the end of the current age. The information in this book has been presented in a form that is readily understandable for lay people so that they can plainly discern what God has said to us in the Bible through his prophets. The material is profoundly unique in its clear and concise chronology of events, challenging a great deal of contemporay thinking.

ISBN 0-933451-44-X

Are We Living In the End Time?
Prophetic Events Destined to Impact Your World
by Rod Hall

Wars! Famine! Earthquakes! Massive destruction around the globe! Are we living in the end time? Many societal trends and world events are taking shape to-day. Are the false prophet and antichrist soon to emerge?

ISBN 0-933451-48-2

ABCs of Globalism
A Vigilant Christians Glossary
by Debra Rae

Do you know what organizations are working together to form a new world order? Unlike any book on today's market, the *ABCs of Globalism* is a single volume reference that belongs in every concerned Christian's home. It allows easy access to over one hundred entries spanning a number or fields–religious, economic, educational, environmental, and more. Each item features an up-to-date overview, coupled with a Biblical perspective.

ISBN 1-56384-140-1

Government by Political Spin
by David J. Turell, M.D.

Political Spin has been raised to a fine art in this country. These highly paid "spin doctors" use sound bites and ambiguous rhetoric to, at best, influence opinions, and at worst, completely mislead the public. *Government by Political Spin* clearly describes the giant PR program used by Washington officials to control the information to American citizens and maintain themselves in power.

ISBN 1-56384-172-X

The Coming Collision
Global Law vs. U.S. Liberties
by James L. Hirsen, Ph.D.

Are Americans' rights being abolished by International Bureaucrats? Global activists have wholeheartedly embraced environmental extremism, international governance, radical feminism, and New Age mysticism with the intention of spreading their philosophies worldwide by using the powerful weight of international law. Noted international and constitutional attorney James L. Hirsen says that a small group of international bureaucrats are devising and implementing a system of world governance that is beginning to adversely and irrevocably affect the lives of everyday Americans.

Paperback ISBN 1-56384-157-6
Hardcover ISBN 1-56384-163-0

Cloning of the American Mind
Eradicating Morality Through Education
by B. K. Eakman

Two-thirds of Americans don't care about honor and integrity in the White House. Why? What does Clinton's hair-splitting definitions have to do with the education establishment? Have we become a nation that can no longer judge between right and wrong?

"Parents who do not realize what a propaganda apparatus the public schools have become should read Cloning of the American Mind *by B. K. Eakman."*

—Thomas Sowell, *New York Post*
September 4, 1998
ISBN 1-56384-147-9

Alien Intervention
The Spiritual Missions of UFOs
by Paul Christopher

Are UFOs mentioned in the Bible? *Alien Intervention* is a thorough treatment of three primary movements: the Occult, the New Age movement, the UFO phenomenon, and their apparent, yet mystifying, connection. *Alien Intervention* is a vital study for anyone fascinated with UFOs and/or Alien contact and challenges the readers beliefs whatever they may be!

ISBN 1-56384-148-7

The Gods Who Walk Among Us
by Thomas R. Horn and Donald C. Jones, Ph.D.

Are we moving toward the Antichrist of the New World Order? Do biblical predictions warn of a revival of paganism and idolatry, which will lead to Armageddon? Authors Thomas Horn and Dr. Donald Jones (Professor of Biblical History) make the startling claim that Zeus, Apollo, Athena, Diana and other mythological deities are alive and well on planet earth!

ISBN 1-56384-161-4

Make Yourself Ready
Preparing to Meet the King
by Harland Miller

Instead of trying to convince readers that one doctrinal position is more valid than another, *Make Yourself Ready* was written to help Christians prepare for the Second Coming. By analyzing Old Testament events, Miller explains how we can avoid Lucifer's age-old deceptions. Scripturally sound and eminently inspiring, *Make Yourself Ready* will create newfound excitement for the return of the Hope of Heaven and show readers how to become truly ready for Judgment Day.

ISBN 0-933451-36-9

Christian Revolution: Practical Answers to Welfare and Addiction
by Arthur Pratt

In *Christian Revolution: Practical Answers to Welfare and Addiction*, Pratt demonstrates that real social and political change starts with radical honesty about the nature of the problem and how we see it. He has called for Congressional action based on his own scientific evidence of what really works in the treatment of addiction. He affirms a renewed faith in Jesus Christ as the inspiration for such action, seeing the church as a servant of our country, not a mentor.

ISBN 1-56384-143-6

Communism, the Cold War, & the FBI Connection
by Herman O. Bly

One out of four people in the world live under Communist rule. If Americans think they are safe from the "red plague," they'd better think again, says author Herman Bly. He will reveal what he's learned in years of counter-intelligence work, and how our country is being lulled into a false sense of security.

ISBN 1-56384-149-5

Dark Cures
Have Doctors Lost Their Ethics?
by Paul deParrie

When traditional ethics were the standard in the field of medicine, one could take comfort in the knowledge that doctors and medical institutions put the health and well-being of the patient above all else. Today, however, pagan ethics have pervaded the professions once properly called "the healing arts, " turning doctors into social engineers and petty gods, and patients into unwitting guinea pigs. The results of this unwise change in direction are horrific and often hard to believe, but also, all too real.

ISBN 1-56384-099-5